Miriam Feinberg Vamosh

Teach It to Your Children:
How Kids Lived
in Bible Days

Teach It to Your Children:
How Kids Lived in Bible Days

Text and research: **Miriam Feinberg Vamosh**
Supervising editor: **Oshri Ofra**
Text editor: **Margery Greenfeld Morgan**
Art director and photography: **Saggie Bernstein**
Graphic design: **Studio Bernstein**
Illustrations: **M. Hass**
Scientific adviser: **Prof. Meir Bar-Ilan**
Educational adviser: **Maya Dubinsky**
Christian education adviser: **Sharon Hopkins**

Acknowledgements:
Judith Abrams; Pnina Arad; Donald Ariel; Rabbi Yisrael Ariel; Etan Ayalon; Yael Barschak (Israel Antiquities Authority – IAA); Gabriela Bijovsky; Malcolm Cartier; CoinArchives.com; Cheri Cowell; Tova Dickstein; Yonatan Dubinsky; EclipseCrossword.com; Eva Marie Everson; Louisa and Karl-Heinz Fleckenetein; Yossi Garfinkel; Avivit Gera (for generous archaeological advice); Clair Hill; David Gal; Haim Gitler; Clare Litt; Abby Lutman; Barbara MacMannus (VRoma); Numismatica Ars Classica; Michal O'Dwyer; Alan Paris; Ramona Richards; Shirley Roth; Barnea Selavan; Orit Shamir; Silk and Honey, Dovrat Hatavor; Shilo Visitor Center; Miki Saban; Leslie Joan Shumka; Kent Wade; David Wexler

Avi Ofra Media, Ltd.
P.O.B. 29241
91292 Jerusalem, Israel
Tel. 972-2-6711888
info@myholyland.net
www.myholyland.net

ISBN 978-965-7574-04-1
PRODUCED IN ISRAEL
DISTRIBUTED BY PALPHOT   WWW.PALPHOT.COM

This book is dedicated to the memory of my beloved parents, Mazal and Asher Ofra
– Avi Ofra

Table of Contents

A Book to Share with the Children You Love

"...do not forget the things your eyes have seen or let them slip from your heart as long as you live. Teach them to your children and to their children after them...." (Deut. 4:9 NIV)

There are precious few Bible stories that mention children, and even fewer that revolve around them. Precisely because these stories are so rare, this book treats each one – like Moses in the bulrushes and his young sister Miriam who saved his life, Hannah who brought her toddler Samuel to serve in the Tabernacle at Shiloh, and the little "lamb" Talitha, whom Jesus healed – as very special gateways of understanding children in Bible times.

The Bible remembers those children because of the amazing experiences they underwent and of course, you'll find all of them in these pages. Children are also a symbol of the Kingdom of God and of God's love (Matt. 18:2-3; Jer. 30:20; Ps. 103:13; 127:3). But you'll also find ordinary children of bygone days, who lived their lives in the Holy Land. Though we don't know their names, we do know a lot about how they lived, and how their parents and grandparents must have raised them with a love for God and God's word.

How do we know about children in Bible times? When it comes to the Hebrew Scriptures, we rely on scholars who have studied the many texts that survived from ancient cultures that mention children and families. For children in Jesus' day, we have a treasure trove of authentic information on family life in the commentaries on the Bible written by Jewish sages of the time. Of course, we don't always know when a certain custom started (only when it was written down), and ancient writings may apply to only one social class or region. But we have woven together every aspect of children's lives in Bible days in the broadest, most authentic way possible to draw a picture of children's lives. At the end, you'll find a list of our sources, so that as your youngsters grow in the Word, they can explore further.

Read this book with your children and grandchildren, nieces and nephews, with the Bible open next to you. You'll instill in them your love of the Holy Land for their whole lives. And you'll discover that across the millennia separating biblical families from your own, that the ancients treasured their offspring just as you do theirs, as a true "heritage of the Lord" (Ps. 127:3 NIV).

Map of the Holy Land

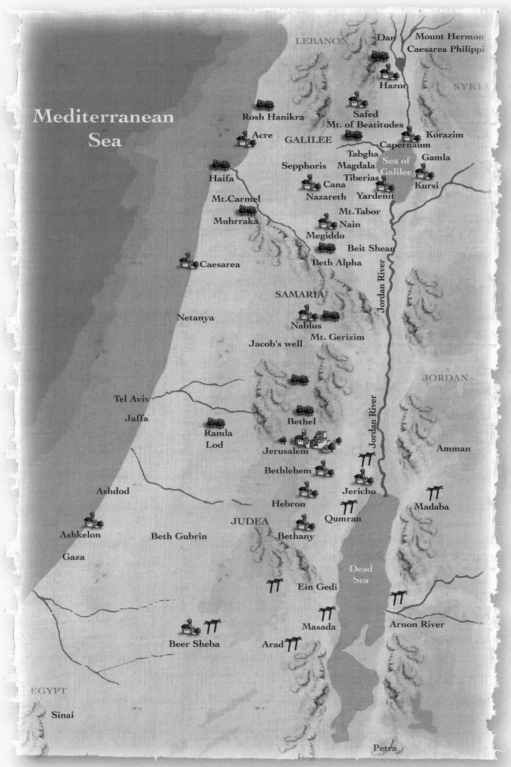

Mediterranean
Sea

LEBANON

Dan
Mount Hermon
Caesarea Philippi

SYRIA

Hazor

Rosh Hanikra
Safed
Mt. of Beatitudes
Korazim

Acre
GALILEE
Capernaum

Tabgha
Gamla

Sepphoris
Magdala
Sea of
Galilee

Haifa
Cana
Tiberias

Mt. Carmel
Nazareth
Yardenit
Kursi

Muhrraka
Mt. Tabor
Nain

Megiddo

Beit Shean

Caesarea
Beth Alpha

SAMARIA

Jordan River

Netanya
Nablus

Jacob's well
Mt. Gerizim

JORDAN

Tel Aviv

Jaffa

Bethel
Jordan River

Ramla
Lod
Amman

Jerusalem

Bethlehem

Ashdod
Jericho
Madaba

Hebron
Qumran

Ashkelon
JUDEA

Beth Gubrin
Bethany

Gaza

Dead
Sea

Ein Gedi

Masada
Arnon River

Beer Sheba
Arad

EGYPT

Sinai

Petra

Many of the places marked on the map are mentioned in this book.

Chapter 1
Household and Family

Starting the Day with the Word

The gray light of morning had not yet peeked in the tiny window high on the wall opposite Sarah's bed when she heard her mother starting up the ladder that led to the rooftop room she shared with her little brother Jacob. But the cock had begun to crow, and leaning on one elbow, Sarah called as softly as she could to Jacob. On this warm spring night, he had taken his sleeping mat out to the flat roof and placed it on the floor there. Grandma, who wove all the mats in their home, never liked when he did that, because it always meant more mending! Jacob was up in a second, rolling up the mat as quickly as an 8-year-old boy could. He managed to drag it back to his room and lay it on his bed before their mother's head appeared at the doorway.

This time, Mama ignored Jacob's morning routine. She was watching Sarah, pleased to see how quickly she had hopped up and was shaking out her reed mat before replacing it over the rope supports of her bed. It was spring and there was lots of work to be done, even before Papa and Jacob went off to the barley field and 11-year-old Sarah took the flocks to the pasture beyond. Besides, in today's morning Bible lesson, Papa had promised them he would answer the riddle he had given them yesterday.

Mama barely had time to check that the children had heard her say good morning – when the baby cried below. She cast a quick glance to make sure their beds were cleared of toys or clutter underneath (she seemed never to tire of telling them how neat a good child's bed should be), and then she started down the ladder again. Papa was waiting for them downstairs for their morning prayer and talk, so they went right over to the clay bowl in the corner of the room and splashed water on their hands, faces and feet and rinsed out their mouths. Then, carefully balancing their **chamber pots**, they climbed down the ladder to begin their day.

From the doorway of the main room, they could see Grandma at the oven in the courtyard, starting the fire with the twigs from the prickly burnet plant Sarah had gathered on her way back from the pasture yesterday. Grandma had the balls of dough lined up next to her, ready to flatten and place on the hot walls of the oven to quickly turn into the bread they would take to the field.

The chickens, as always, were running around their corner of the courtyard, right around Grandma and the little cloud of white smoke already rising from the oven. She didn't shoo them away – the smoke's good for them, Sarah had heard Grandma say every morning of her life.

Grandma made do with an absentminded smile at the children as they passed her with their chamber pots on the way to the little stream about 20 minutes walk from their home. Their first hug of the day would come on their return, when she handed them a steaming cup of tea made from the sage plant and a few sweet, dried dates from the rooftop jar. That simple breakfast would hold them until they unpacked their midday meal, Jacob in the field with his father and Sarah in the pasture, with only the little flock of sheep and goats for company.

The children ducked into the main room of the house, where Papa had already wrapped the leather straps of his *tefillin* around his arm and hand, with the little black box with its Bible verses firmly fixed on his forehead. They stopped and stood quietly as Papa got to their favorite part: "Fix these words of mine in your hearts and minds; tie them as symbols on your hands and bind them on your foreheads. Teach them to your children, talking about them when you sit at home and when you walk along the road, when you lie down and when you get up. Write them on the doorframes of your houses and on your gates, so that your days and the days of your children may be many in the land that the

8

Lord swore to give your forefathers, as many as the days that the heavens are above the earth."*

Even on the busiest days, Papa always found time for their daily Bible lesson. Even today, although the sun was already up and the rest of the ripe barley had to be gathered in as soon as possible – you never knew when storm clouds might roll in and ruin the harvest. But they settled in to find out the answer to the riddle Papa had given them both, yesterday morning in the barley field. Mama had gone out with the flocks so that Sarah could hear it, too.

"When do you work hardest when you're not working at all?" he had asked them. Then he had sat them both down and told them to stay put in one corner of the field, from when the sun first began to warm the field of ripe grain until it climbed to the top of the sky. Meanwhile, Papa, hard at work with his laborers, didn't let them help at all. So the golden grain in their corner stood tall as the rest was cut down and tied into bundles. "Well, children, do you know the answer to the riddle?" he asked, flashing a secret smile at Sarah, who already did know. She remembered this lesson from last year, but Papa had made her promise not to tell her little brother.

They both shook their heads, Sarah playing along. "Today we're going to remember Ruth," Papa said, and began to recite from memory Ruth's beloved words to Naomi: " 'let me go into the field and pick up the leftover grain from those in whose eyes I find favor.'"

"You'll hear the whole story soon enough, in synagogue, on Pentecost – it's only six days away. But for now, children, remember – we don't harvest everything in our field – we always leave some behind for poor people, who, like Ruth and Naomi, may have no one to look after them."

"But we didn't do anything all morning! What's so hard about that, Papa?" Jacob demanded, pulling at his father's outer robe, which he had already put on as he got ready to leave.
"Well, it's hard work to give up something you want for yourself to someone else, now, isn't it?"
The children nodded gravely as Papa said, "All right, children, Mama is ready to send us off."

Stopping for their hug from Grandma, who was getting ready to take her place at the loom for a morning of weaving, the children left their courtyard for the lane in front of their house. Mama was standing beside the donkey she had saddled with their food for the day. Papa's and Jacob's food would stay with them on the donkey, together with the scythes, the knives for cutting down the grain, and the other tools they would use in the harvest. Sarah shouldered the small sack containing her food as her mother fastened the flat jar of water at her waist. And off went the little family to gather in their harvest and watch over their sheep and goats.

What does that mean?

Chamber pot: Before people had toilets or running water in their homes (and today in many places in the world) people had a special pot in their bedroom (chamber is another word for room) that they had to empty in the morning.

Tefillin: A Hebrew word related to the word for prayer. This custom comes from Deut. 6:6-9 and Deut. 11:19-21, which says to bind the word of God "between our eyes" and "on our hands." Jewish people do that by putting Bible verses in a special little box with straps, the Tefillin, and tying it onto their hand and head during daily prayers.

✱ Deut. 11:18-21

Life in the Biblical Family

"In the very heart of your house, your children like olive plants all around your table" (Ps 128:3 NKJV)

You can imagine the people in the story that began this chapter – Sarah, Jacob and their baby brother Isaac, their parents and grandmother – living in a small village in the days of Jesus. Perhaps their home was in Capernaum or Korazim or Bethsaida in the Galilee, where Jesus often visited, or in Katzrin in the Golan Heights, where ancient houses have been rebuilt so visitors can see how people lived. Perhaps the family in our story lived in a village near Jerusalem, like Bethlehem, where Jesus and King David were born.

This little family of farmers worked very hard, all of them busy with their own tasks so the family could make its living. They even built their house themselves, out of stone or maybe bricks made out of mud, sometimes covered with plaster.

They probably didn't have as much space in their house or as many rooms as some people do today. Only rich people had houses with lots of rooms, and that gave them more privacy, especially for the women of the family.

Some houses in Bible times had two stories, with the bedrooms on the second floor. Do you remember the Bible story of the prophet Elijah who saved the life of a sick little boy? He brought the boy to the upstairs room where he was staying and said a prayer (1 Kings 17:19).

In places like Capernaum you can see how small the rooms of the houses were, and that the houses stood very close together. When Jacob and baby Isaac from our story grew up and got married, they'd probably build their house right next to their parents. When Sarah got married, she'd go to live with her husband near his parents.

You didn't have to be rich to sleep in a bed like Sarah and Jacob did (although only rich people had pillows). Instead of mattresses like we have nowadays, they stretched ropes across the bed frame very tight, and laid a mat like Jacob's over it. Or they had a sort of mattress filled with dried plants, called rushes, which grow by lakes and streams.
Wooden benches and tables were made by carpenters, which the Gospel of Mark (6:3) says

Painted clay model of a house, made many thousands of years ago at Tel Arad
(IAA)

Empress Diva Faustia sitting on her throne and handing out food to families
(Courtesy Numismatica Ars Classica, Auction 54 Lot 1152)

This bed, in Sturbridge Village, Massachusetts, was made with ropes to support the mattress, as in Jesus' day
(Courtesy of Aaron Vamosh)

Did your mother or your father ever wish you a good night's sleep by telling you to "sleep tight"? That goes all the way back to Bible days, when people were most comfortable when the ropes under their mat or mattress were pulled nice and tight!

Ancient people made butter by attaching ropes to such a container filled with milk and swinging it on a stand (IAA)

Ruins of a house in Capernaum, which was the center of Jesus' ministry

An olive press in Capernaum

Remains of an Israelite house at Megiddo (Armageddon) (Rev. 16:16)

Jesus was. Cradles for babies were another common piece of furniture. But unlike today, the cradle was where the baby slept only during the day – at night, a baby like little Isaac in our story would sleep in his parents' bed. In the Milestones in Life chapter you'll learn more about the baby Jesus' special cradle, the manger, and you'll even learn how to make one.

Because it's so warm in the Holy Land most of the time, people could do lots of things in their courtyard or on their roof that in colder places you'd have to stay indoors to do – like eating and sleeping! Cooking and baking, for instance, were done outdoors, the way Sarah and Jacob's grandmother did in our story. Later on in this book, you'll find out how to bake bread the way they did it in the Bible.

Animals, like chickens and geese, lived in the courtyard. Two thousand years ago, in Roman times, a man named Columella wrote a cookbook. He wrote that people thought the smoke from the oven in the courtyard was healthy for the chickens. There were also very big jars in the courtyard that Sarah would have to help her mother keep filled with water they would bring every day from the stream. The clay jars had to have tight covers on them so no snakes could get in!

The roof was flat and made of straw and mud that was packed down very hard with a special stone roller attached to wooden handles. People stored lots of things on their roof. In the Bible we read about Rehab, the woman who saved the spies God sent to see the Promised Land. She kept flax – a plant used to make linen cloth – on her roof (Josh. 2:6).

Families also passed the time together on the rooftop, which was pleasant and breezy at night. And it was a very special place to pray, like Peter did on the rooftop of Simon the Tanner in Joppa (Acts 10:9).

The floors in a simple countryside house like Sarah's and Jacob's were made out of earth that was packed down very hard. Every day you'd have to sweep the floor and sprinkle water on it to keep the dust down. But you had to make sure all that sprinkling didn't cause a plant to sprout if you dropped a seed on your floor by accident.

Archaeologists know what houses looked like back in the early days of the Bible from the remains they have found as they dig into the earth. Houses were square or rectangular in shape and mostly had four rooms – two in the back, and one on each side, with a courtyard in the middle. Sometimes farm animals would be kept there, or in one of the side rooms. The Bible describes a house like that, where the woman sometimes called "the witch of Endor" lived. She hosted King Saul in her home and brought a calf to cook from a room in her house (1 Sam. 28:24). In Jerusalem's City of David, you can see the remains of a house like that dating back thousands of years, to the time of the prophet Jeremiah.

The patriarchs Abraham, Isaac and Jacob and their wives and children lived in tents. Some people still live in tents if, like Abraham, they mainly make their living grazing animals and have to move from place to place to make sure the animals always have enough food and water. This was not like a tent you use for camping in the backyard. It was much bigger, and the walls were woven by the mother, grandmother or big sister from scratchy goat hair. But just like when you go camping, they could also take their tent apart quickly. They would fold it up and put it on the back of their camel or their donkey, and move on to the next place where there was food and water for their animals.

The patriarchs had more than one wife, and each wife had her own tent (Gen. 31:33). The Israelites had a tent, called the Tent of Meeting, where they worshipped God (Ex. 29:42). If you lived in those days, sometimes your mother or your father would go to the entrance of the tent to worship the Lord, and sometimes you could go with them when everyone in your tribe was called – but only the priests would be allowed inside. Still, Samuel was only three years old when his mother brought him to be the helper to Eli the priest at the Tent of Meeting in Shiloh.

Your family is your household

In Bible days, your home and your family together were called your "household." People lived with their parents, their grandparents, sometimes aunts or big sisters who did not have a husband or children. If you were wealthy and had servants, they were also part of your household.

The love of parents for their children was so important that when the Bible describes God's love for us, it says God is like a father or a mother. Jeremiah said God looked at his people as "my son, my darling child" (Jer. 31:20 NLT) – even when that child did things wrong. The prophet Isaiah (66:13) said God comforts us "like a mother comforts her child," and we hope all children know how good that feels. Jesus said he felt like a mother hen taking care of her chicks (Matt. 23:37). The Apostle Paul says he took care of the new church gently, "like a mother caring for her little children" (1 Thess. 2:7 NCV).

Just like today, parents had to make sure their children had enough to eat. Jesus said: "If your children ask for bread, which of you would give them a stone?" (Matt. 7:9 NCV) (See page 120).

Small statue of a woman nursing her baby, found at Maresha (Josh. 15:24, 2 Chron. 11:8), about 2,300 years old (IAA)

Many parents came to Jesus to ask them to heal their children, like the man who came to Jesus after the transfiguration (Matt. 17:14-17), the man whose son was sick in Capernaum (John 4:46) and a woman from Tyre (Mark 7:25). You can picture your parents doing the same for you.

You might live in or near the household where you were born your whole life long. Rachel and Leah, for example, were sisters who grew up together and both became the wives of Jacob. As you can imagine, sometimes brothers, like Ishmael, who teased Isaac (Gen. 21:9), did not get along, especially when they had different mothers. Sometimes they had to live apart for their whole lives as a result. If families lost their mother or their father, the remaining parent would try to marry again as soon as possible, so you would have usually had lots of new brothers and sisters before you knew it.

The most important duty children had, and still have, was to honor their parents, which is what the Fifth Commandment teaches (Ex. 20:12). Honoring your parents means to respect and obey them. Paul the Apostle speaks especially to children about this commandment when he said: "Children, obey your parents as the Lord wants, because this is the right thing to do. The command says, 'Honor your father and mother.' This is the first command that has a promise with it – 'Then everything will be well with you, and you will have a long life on the earth.'" (Eph. 6:1-2 NCV).

A woman spinning thread, next to a little girl, in the ancient village of Samoa near Hebron (Seffi Ben Joseph, courtesy of the Eretz Israel Museum, Tel Aviv)

Activities

3

Cooking Pot
To cook food over an open fire or on a stove (Gen. 15:17)
With two handles

6

Huge Jars
To store lots of wheat, barley or other grain, or lentils
Very big, no lid

1

Jug
To hold liquids (water, wine, oil)
Gen. 24:14; Sam. 26:11 NLT
Narrow neck; two handles

4

Bowl
To serve food (Matt. 26:23; Mark 4:21)
Just like you use today

Courtesy of I. Beit-Areh

2

Juglet
To hold perfume, medicine, oil or other expensive items (John 12:3)
Small, with a little opening

5

Big Jar
To hold wine for a sea journey, placed in a holder so it wouldn't spill; at home they could lean it against a wall
Very big with pointed bottom

7

Very Big Bowl
To hold wheat, barley or other grain
A wide bowl that usually had a lid

In the picture above, you can see different kinds of ceramic containers people used in their homes in ancient times. Draw an arrow from the name of the container to the right container in the picture.

Answer on page 144

See more activities for this chapter in the pocket at the back of this book!

The roots of this family tree remind us that we should think of the first people in the Bible as our ancestors. Write your name and the names of other people in your family in the branches of this tree, or make one like it and hang it up at home.

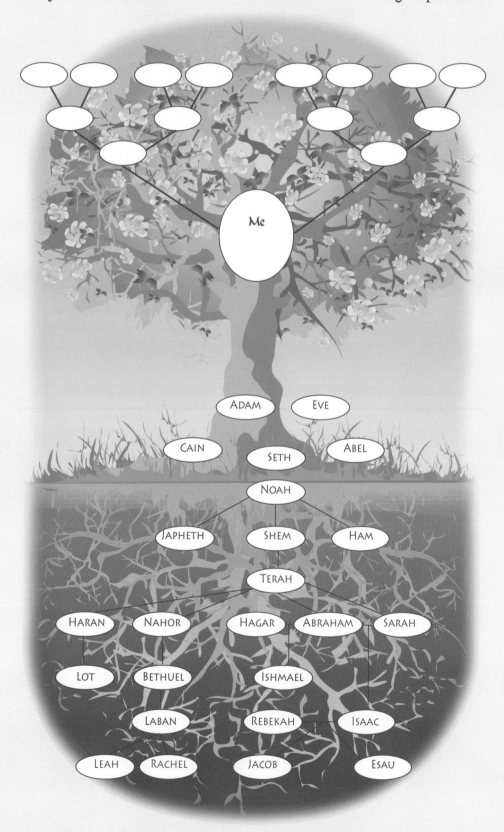

Chapter 2
Education

Zira's First Day at School

This morning, Zira was happy he was holding Mama's hand beneath the folds of her **mantle**. He was seven years old, and it was his first day of school. He chattered away as they walked up the street to the synagogue. Mama squeezed his hand back warmly. "Today is the day you've been waiting for!" she said.

"Of course I have," said Zira, speaking seriously. His older brother Joshua had started studying *Mikra*, the first five books of the Bible, when he was five years old, and he sometimes teased Zira for still being at home in the mornings with Mama and Grandmama. And although their oldest brother Jonathan, who was 15, now worked with their father in his carpentry shop, he went to the synagogue every afternoon to study with the rest of **Korazim's** smartest boys.

"Papa says the rabbis say when a boy is 5, he should start studying Mikra," Zira said. Mama sighed. She repeated what she had told him every time he brought this up, which he seemed to do at least twice a day – when his brothers left for school, and when they came back. "Yes, dear, some do say that. But I have heard others say that children should start school when they are ready. And now, Zira, you are finally ready!"

"How do you know I'm ready, Mama? I think I have good answers to share, but I'm afraid I might say something wrong if the teacher asks me a question!" Zira said.

"Just last week in the synagogue I heard the rabbis talking about that very thing," Mama answered. "They were discussing whether we should always think up something new to say to God when we pray, or say the same prayer each time so we don't make a mistake. A young rabbi – who has the same name as you, Zira – said just what you said now: 'I'm afraid of making a mistake.' And do you know what one of the older rabbis, said to him?"

"What?" Zira wondered.

"He said not to worry about mistakes, and that we shouldn't be afraid of saying something new!"

With that, they arrived at the synagogue door. Mama handed Zira a little linen bag containing the dates and flat bread he would eat later in the morning. Then she handed him a surprise – a small package tied to her belt that held a cake of nuts, figs, honey and spices that she usually served only on the Sabbath. "God bless you, my son," she smiled. "Have a sweet first day of school!

Zira knew the synagogue very well; everyone in Korazim, mothers, fathers, uncles, aunts, and children, gathered there every Sabbath to hear the Bible read and listen to the preacher. But today, as every weekday, the mats were rolled out on the floor for the children to sit on, and the teacher was waiting for them, sitting in the teacher's seat, called the Moses Seat.

As he took a place in the second of the two rows, Zira was thinking about what Mama had said about thinking up new things – especially when he spotted the reed stick in the teacher's hand. His brothers had already told him about that stick, saying the teacher wasn't afraid to use it on students, even when they were acting just a little bit silly.

In a fine, loud voice, the teacher slowly recited a verse from Genesis, and all the boys repeated it after him. Zira chimed in, because his father had already taught him this verse. "Then God said, 'Let us make human beings in our image and likeness.'" After many repetitions, the teacher asked a question: "What does it mean for us to be made in God's image?"

Silence. It seemed like everyone felt the same way Zira did. Who would dare to answer first? Finally, Samuel, his younger cousin and next-door neighbor, piped up. "It means God looks like us, only much bigger!" he said. Some of the boys snickered at the thought that we could know how big God was. The teacher glared at them, and then nodded kindly at Samuel. Another boy's idea was that "we are like God because we help people and God helps people." This also got a silent nod from the teacher.

The teacher looked straight at Zira, as if he could feel his bright-eyed new pupil wanted to say something.
"Yes, Zira?" the teacher said.
Trying to keep his voice from shaking, Zira said: "We are like God because we can speak, and so can God."
The teacher paused for a moment, and Zira got a little nervous.
The teacher rose, and gave a little bow to the boy and said with a smile: "A fine answer! For did not the Holy One blessed be He create the world with words?"

Zira would always remember his teacher's words of praise on his first day at school and for the rest of his life, they helped him find the courage to speak out.

What does that mean?

Mantle: An outer cloak. Jewish men at the time of Jesus had special fringes hanging from this cloak (Num. 15:37-40).
Mikra: The Hebrew word for the first five books of the Bible.
Korazim: A village near the Sea of Galilee (Matt. 11:21) (see map on page 5).

A woman is helping a little girl read in this wall painting from a wealthy home in Roman Pompeii.
(By authorization of the Italian Ministry for Cultural Heritage and Environment, reproduction prohibited)

Learning and Studying in Bible Days

"Train children how to live right, and when they are old, they will not change" (Prov. 22:6 NCV)

Papyrus plants,
from which ancient paper was made

In ancient times, not all children went to school like Zira – many were home-schooled by their parents (like some children are today). But the most important thing for children of the Bible was to make sure they got an education.

Moses told the people he was leading to the Promised Land that he knew their children would one day ask them: "What is the meaning of the laws, commands, and rules the Lord our God gave us?" (Deut. 6:20 NCV). And so he told them it was their job to teach all the laws to their children,

The Bible also told children they should pay attention to their parents: "My child, listen to your father's teaching and do not forget your mother's advice" (Prov. 1:8 NCV). Like today, the most important thing parents could teach their children was to learn from the Bible how to be a good person. That is what the verse from the book of Proverbs at the top of this section means – to raise your children to be good people. The Bible was – and still is – the best place to learn all about these things. In fact, one Hebrew word for the first part of the Bible is Torah, which means teaching.

Torah scroll
(Shutterstock)

In Jesus' time, everyone's main education was listening to the Torah being read in the synagogue on the Sabbath. We know there were schools already in the time of Paul, who mentions "a teacher of babes" (Rom. 2:20) (babes meant young children).

Among wealthy people in Jesus' day, both boys and girls were taught at home. At first, schools were only for children whose parents could afford to pay the teacher, but then it was decided that all boys, rich or poor, should go to school. Girls sometimes also learned to read, but at that time, many people thought girls should stay home and only learn what they needed to know to run their homes when they grew up, skills like spinning and sewing.

An inkwell from the City of David in
Jerusalem (IAA)

The word "school" is not mentioned in the Old Testament. But in the time of the prophet Nehemiah about 2,400 years ago, it is believed that people thought children could begin studying the Bible whenever they were able to understand it and to celebrate various holidays the way the Bible said to do (Neh. 8:2).

Five tiny ancient Hebrew letters a child may have scratched on a palace step in the biblical city of Lachish, dating about 1,400 years ago (Josh. 10:3; 2 Chron. 32:9) (Courtesy of Wellcome Library, London)

Even before Nehemiah's time, we think the 70 sons of King Ahab might have had teachers, which the Bible calls by a special Hebrew word – *omnim* (2 Kings 10:1, 5), which Bibles in the English language usually translate as "guardians." We also think the prophet Isaiah knew about teachers, because he says people made fun of the way he tried to teach them to do right. They felt like he was treating them like a schoolteacher treats children: "He tells us everything over and over again, a line at a time a little here, a little there" (Isa. 28:10 NLT).

The first school mentioned in Scripture might have been in the book of Ecclesiasticus, a book of good advice that is something like the Book of Proverbs. Written around 300 years before the birth of Jesus by a man named Ben Sirah, it is studied mainly by Christians who are Catholics or Eastern Orthodox. In that book it says: "Draw near to me those who are untaught and lodge [live] in my school." We read that schools were founded because people were worried that children who did not have fathers would have no way of learning Bible. So they decided there would be teachers in every town and that children would start school at the age of six or seven. One ancient source said there were to be no more than 25 children in a class, or the teacher had to hire an assistant.

Pillars in the synagogue at Korazim (Luke 10:13), a town where Jesus performed miracles. Children in Jesus' day often went to school in their synagogues

Lessons could be held almost anywhere, indoors or out. In a book called the *Infancy Gospel of Thomas*, there is a legend that when Jesus was a boy, he came across a group of students and a teacher in the marketplace. Paul's teacher, Rabbi Gamliel, had a school in his home. These schools must have been pretty noisy places, because the leaders of the Jewish people said that even if someone complained they couldn't sleep because of the noise your pupils were making, you could still open a school in your neighborhood.

When people first started thinking about when to start teaching their children the things the Bible said to do, like celebrating the holidays, they decided children could do anything the Bible said, as soon as they could manage to do it. During the Feast of Tabernacles, for example, if children knew how to wave the palm branch people brought to the Temple to celebrate the holiday (Lev. 23:40), they should wave the branch themselves.

A copy of the ancient seat for the preacher in the Korazim synagogue

But after the time of Jesus, people seemed to believe that there was a right age for each kind of learning. Children should begin to learn the Bible at five, they said, and then go on to learn things that were harder to understand at age 10, and then even harder things at age 15. The people of Jesus' time believed that fathers had to teach their sons Bible and a trade – and also how to swim.

Fathers also taught their boys farming or other skills so they could make their living when they got older and started their own families. In addition to cooking and weaving, mothers taught their daughters how to raise and dry fresh fruits and vegetables so they could serve them months later.

In Jesus' day, young men and some young women could learn how to be doctors by studying with an older doctor, starting at around age 14 and completing their studies at around age 18. In Rome, most young men who wanted to be lawyers started law school at 16 and finished when they were about 21.

A mezuzah

Because Jesus was a carpenter (Mark 6:3) and so was Joseph (Matt. 13:55), we imagine that Joseph taught Jesus his trade. From stories about children around the time of Jesus we can imagine that Jesus probably started working with Joseph no later than the age of 13.

A Roman historian, Suetonius, who was born in the same century as Jesus, taught his grandsons the alphabet (he wanted them to copy his own handwriting), as well as how to swim. A famous statesman named Cato the Elder, who lived in Rome about 250 years before Jesus was born, writes that he taught his son the alphabet, laws, sports, horseback riding and how to swim down waterfalls.

Many wealthy Greeks and Romans who were not Jews or Christians used slaves for teachers. But in the world of Jesus and later, people wanted to teach their children themselves. One rabbi wrote that teachers were like those "who lead many to righteousness like the stars forever" (Daniel 12:3 NLT).

English letter	Picture	What does it look like?	Early writing	Modern writing	Name of Hebrew letter
A		ox head		א	alef
B		house		ב	bet
G		foot		ג	gimel
D		fish		ד	dalet
H		man calling		ה	heh
W		mace		ו	vav
Z	?	?		ז	zayin
H		fence?		ח	het
T	?	spindle		ט	tet
Y		arm		י	yod
K		palm		כ	kaf
L		shepherd's staff		ל	lamed
M		water		מ	mem
N		snake		נ	nun
S	?	shield?		ס	samekh
A		eye		ע	ayin
P		mouth?		פ	peh
S/Z		plant		צ	tzadi
Q		setting or rising sun		ק	qof
R		head of man		ר	resh
S		teeth?		ש	shin
T		owner's mark		ת	taf

The ancient and modern Hebrew alphabets

Teachers encouraged students to ask questions, like Jesus did of the rabbis in the Temple (Luke 2:46), but also demanded that their pupils memorize the Bible, which they did by saying or singing it out loud. In the Holy Land today, you can still hear some children chanting this way as they learn.

Teachers also taught their pupils how to say blessings like the prayer after meals. So schools were very important to the family's life of faith.

In ancient times, books were very expensive because they were handwritten by scribes on materials that had to be especially prepared – and so most people did not own them.
If you wanted to know what a book said, you had to listen to someone who had read it. And so, people must have understood that a lot in life depended on whether you could speak well.

You had to listen very closely to your teacher to know how to pronounce words correctly. One ancient story tells about a community whose teacher was very hard on the children, and they were thinking about firing him. But he was so good at pronouncing words, they decided to let him go on teaching.

At the time of Jesus, most people spoke a language called Aramaic in their everyday lives. There are some words in Aramaic in the Gospels. For example, when Jesus spoke to Jairus' little daughter to make her well when she was sick, he said to her: "Talitha, kumi," which means "lamb, get up" (Mark 5:41). In those days, Hebrew was the language people used when they prayed, and when they read or listened to the Bible.

A teacher from Rome named Quintilian, who lived around the same time as Paul the Apostle, made up children's games to help them have fun while they learned the alphabet. One of his ideas was giving students letters made out of ivory to play with so they could learn to recognize their shapes.

Children had to be very respectful of their teachers. They had to stand up when the teacher came into the room, and they were never allowed to say the teacher was wrong. The teacher was a kind of representative of the parent, so the pupils had to show them the same honor as they would their parents.

Punishments in Bible Times

Earlier in the history of the Israelites, the law said that anyone who curses their parents or a son who disobeyed his father (Ex. 21:17, Deut. 21:18-21) could be put to death. The biblical book of Proverbs says parents should correct their children's behavior (Prov. 19:18) and spank their children if they had to (Prov. 23:13-14). The Bible does not talk much about this subject, but the rules that people lived by in later times, around the time of Jesus for example, mention parents spanking their children quite a bit. Still, these sources also made rules that protected children from being hurt by their parents. Unlike today, in those days, teachers could also hit their students, and they probably used a reed stick, like the one the teacher held in our little story.

Rich and Poor

If you went to a school that had its own teacher, it seems likely that your parents and the other people in the town would have paid the teacher, because the Book of Proverbs says "Wisdom is the most important thing; so get wisdom. If it costs everything you have, get understanding" (Prov. 4:7 NCV). We also read about a teacher who did not let a poor student pay anything. In the beginning, poor children did not go to school, but later, a famous rabbi named Hillel said that everyone, no matter how rich or how poor, should go to school.

Writing

In Bible days, the most important reason to learn how to read was so people could understand God's word. The Bible says people should write the Bible verses on their doors and gates to their houses (Deut. 6:9) to remind them of God's teachings. People would write down Bible verses and put them in a little box called a mezuzah (see page 21). This word actually means "doorpost" in Hebrew. But it also means the box in which Jewish people place certain verses of Scripture on the doorframe of their home.

If you lived in Bible times, you would probably learn to read long before you learned to write. That's because learning how to write also meant learning how to prepare the material you wrote on and how to make your own pens and ink, and that was hard work for little children.

People probably first learned the alphabet by tracing letters on stone tablets. Schools for scribes – people who wrote for a living – were first started in a land called Mesopotamia, where Abraham was from, but long before his time. These schools were called "houses of tablets" because people first wrote by scratching the words on stone with a special instrument called a chisel, or on clay tablets.

In the story of the birth of John the Baptist, the Gospel of Luke tells us that Zechariah, John's father, couldn't speak when it was time to give the baby his name, so he wrote the baby's name on a "tablet" (Luke 1:63). This may have been what we'd call nowadays a notebook that you could carry with you just in case you needed to write something down. These ancient "notebooks" were made of two pieces of wood covered with wax that you would scratch into with a special pen called a stylus. Or your "notebook" could have been a smooth piece of wood that you wrote on in ink.

Alef ahava – love

Bet bayit – house

Gimel gamal – camel

Dalet delet – door

Heh har – mountain

Vav vilon – curtain

Zayin zoog – couple

Het hamor – donkey

Tet teneh – basket

Yod Yerushalayim – Jerusalem

Kaf cad – pitcher

Lamed laila – night

Mem magal – sickle

Nun nahash – snake

Samekh sulam – ladder

Ayin ayin – eye

Peh peh – mouth

Tzadi tsipor – bird

Qof qof – monkey

Resh ro'eh – shepherd

Shin/Sin sadeh – field

Tav tamar date – fruit

23

This inscription was written in ink on a broken piece of a large clay jar. A 17-year-old volunteer found it in 2008 during the archaeological dig at ruins called Khirbet Qeiyafa in the Elah Valley where the Bible says David fought Goliath. The writing is from around 3,000 years ago, when the alphabet still used pictures for letters. For example, look at the letter with a circle around a dot, near the middle of the first line. That's an *ayin*. It means "eye" in Hebrew, and it looks like an eye. Now look for another picture-letter: a squiggly upside-down line – you'll see a few of these. That's the letter *mem*, the first letter in the Hebrew word for water. And what does it look like? A wave! Archaeologists say this is the earliest Hebrew inscription ever found. They are still studying its meaning, but they think it uses some of the same language as the ancient Hebrew Bible

Photo above and below: Israel Exploration Society courtesy of Prof. Yosef Garfinkel, Khirbet Qeiyafa Project, Hebrew University of Jerusalem

Khirbet Qeiyafa, the ruined town where the ancient inscription you see above was found. Experts are very excited about this site, because they think the ruins are from a biblical town called Shaaraim (1 Sam. 17:52) mentioned at the end of the story of David's victory over Goliath

People used to write on lots of different materials. Pieces of broken clay pots were like the "scratch paper" of Bible times. Writing material was also made out of a plant called papyrus. When you say the word papyrus, does it remind you of anything? That's right – it gave us the English word "paper."

The Bible you read today in church and at home is printed on paper. Papyrus is first mentioned in a story of a man named Wen Amon who traveled to Phoenicia on the coast north of the Holy Land (Isa. 23:11, Mark 7:26, Acts 21:2), over 3,000 years ago. He brought papyrus to use as payment for some cedar trees he was buying from the king of a place called Gebal. That city later became a center for selling papyrus and its name was changed to Byblos, which gives us our word "Bible."

In ancient times, the Bible was written on scrolls made of special leather. Today, Jewish people praying in synagogues still read the first five books of the Bible from a Torah scroll handwritten on leather (see page 20).

Around the time of Jesus, people sometimes wrote on an olive leaf or a cow's horn, and God told the prophet Ezekiel to write a special message on wood (Ezek. 37:16-17). Writing on wax was a good idea, because you could "erase it" and start again. The book of Job mentions a pen made out of iron used to write on another metal, lead (Job 19:24). The book of Jeremiah also mentions a pen.

In the New Testament, when John wrote to his friend Gaius, "I have many things to write to you, but I do not want to use pen and ink" (3 John 1:13, NCV), he was probably writing with a reed pen. His "ink" was probably made by mixing water and soot, the black dust that comes from burning wood. People also had red ink, which they could make by crushing rocks that contained a reddish mineral called iron oxide.

Archaeologists have found many lists of words and letters carved into stone in different places in the Bible lands. One of these, listing the months of the year and the farming tasks that went with them, was found in a place near Jerusalem called Gezer (Josh. 10:33, 1 Kings 9:17), which people can visit when they are in the Holy Land. In another ancient city called Lachish (Josh. 10:32), archaeologists found letters of the alphabet had been scratched into the steps of the governor's house. We can imagine a little boy practicing his writing there before a guard stopped him!

Scribes were considered very important people, especially the ones who made copies of the Bible, because they knew the Bible very well and could teach it. However, the Bible says scribes did not always teach people the right thing (Jer. 8:8).

In Bible days, writing quickly was considered a compliment to a writer. The Bible, in the original Hebrew, says Ezra the Scribe was "quick" (Ezra 7:6; Ps. 45:1). But even good scribes sometimes made mistakes. Since they didn't have erasers in those days, if a scribe who was copying a Bible scrolls forgot a letter, he would write the missing letter above the line. If he wrote the wrong letter, he could scrape it off with a little knife.

Activities

Find and color the Hebrew letters hidden in this picture of Noah's Ark.
(First study the letters on page 22.) The answer is on page 144.

Write your name in Hebrew inside this scroll.
(Look for the sounds of the letter on page 22)

Chapter 3
Work

Lucky Lucian

As I grew up, I sometimes wished I were Lucian, instead of just being a slave in his household. Yes, I'm the one who brings Lucian his washing water in the morning, sews up his torn clothing, brings his meals and plays stickball or marbles with him (or whatever game he wishes, whenever he wishes it).

We are the same age, we both have seen 12 summers. I even learned to read and write along with Lucian, because my father, who is also a slave, was his teacher. Lucian was able to have his schooling, just like the wealthy boys of our town, Samosata, on the banks of the Euphrates River in today's Turkey. And Lucian's sister could spend her days weaving alongside her mother in the women's quarters. Lucian's mother and sister almost never left the house. They had two maidservants who went to the market for them whenever they needed new wool to spin into thread and bought the food and prepared the meals when Lucian's mother was arranging a banquet for Lucian's father's friends.

I knew Lucian would get into trouble after our school days were over this year. I could tell from the way he got into trouble while we were both still students! Each day, when my father had left us to practice writing our Greek letters, he would scrape some of the wax from writing tablets. Little by little, he gathered enough wax to make several small balls, which he would ask me to hide in the straw of my mattress and bring him at our playtime. Then, he would form them into marvelous figures of men, women, cows and horses. One day, he even made a likeness of me, which I kept in my mattress and loved to look at sometimes, after Lucian went away.

I remember the day when Lucian's father decided he had had enough schooling, and it was time to learn a trade. His father's friends entered the dining room and reclined at the table. I heard everything they said as I walked in and out of the room, refilling their plates and pouring more wine into their cups. "It's time to teach the boy a trade," Lucian's father announced. Each man made a suggestion – one suggested he learn how to make nails, another to comb sheep's wool and get it ready to use as thread, another even said Lucian would make a good musician. But then, Lucian's

father turned to Lucian's mother's brother, who was a master stone-carver, and said: "The boy loves to carve, even in the wax he thinks we do not know he scrapes from his school tablets. Take the lad and teach him how to carve stone!" All the men agreed that this would be a good way for Lucian to earn a living, and he would learn everything he needed in a few years' time.

A few days later, everyone was there to say goodbye as Lucian's uncle came to take him to his workshop as his apprentice. Lucian was very proud of himself. "When I come back, I'll bring you a stone carving of your face!" he boasted to me.

What a shock we all got when Lucian returned home the very next day! And he was crying, too. "Uncle gave me a flat piece of stone to carve a frame around the edges, and I was supposed to follow the lines someone had already carved in the stone," I heard him tell his mother. "He handed me a hammer and chisel and showed me how to hold it, but that was it. I guess he thought the job wasn't too hard for a beginner," Lucian continued.

Well-begun is half-done Lucian said the uncle had told him. But poor Lucian discovered that morning the difference between what a little fruit knife did to wax and what a chisel did to stone. "I tapped on it once with the hammer, just to try it out – and my very first stroke broke the tablet," he told his mother in tears. He showed his mother a bruise where his uncle had beaten him with a stick. The next time Lucian's uncle came to their house, all across the courtyard and into the kitchen we could hear Lucian's mother scolding her brother for laying a hand on Lucian.

By the next day, everyone in the household was talking about "Lucky Lucian." Why so lucky? Because the boy came to his father that morning, and began to tell him about a dream he had the night before, that he would become a great writer. On the spot, his father agreed to let him try. Calling his friends together again, Lucian's father asked if anyone knew of a scribe in the law courts to whom his son could be apprenticed, and off Lucian went that very week. Eventually, Lucian's dream of writing really did come true and the whole city of Samosata was talking about their most famous son. When I followed in my father's footsteps as a teacher and taught Lucian's children, I would tell them how their famous father had begun – as a sculptor of wax balls!

This story is loosely based on the opening chapter of the autobiography of Lucian of Samosata, a writer who was born around 120 AD in a city on the Euphrates River.

What does that mean?

"Well-begun is half-done": If you start out a job right, you've already done half the work. An expression by the Greek philosopher Aristotle, who lived about 2,400 years ago.

Mosaic of a young kitchen slave, around 300 years after Jesus' day, Rome
(The Hermitage, St. Petersburg)

> "Joseph, a young man of seventeen, was tending the flocks with his brothers…" (Gen. 37:2 NIV)

The story you just read is based on the life of a real boy named Lucian, who lived about 1,800 years ago. Lucian's family had enough money to have servants and to give their son a good education. But even Lucian had to begin working – or learning a trade – when he was around 12 years old. That is what children once did (and still do, in some places in the world), going all the way back to Bible times.

As you learned in the chapter on family life, especially on the farm, everyone worked together to get everything done (the same is true in farming families today). The prophet Jeremiah tells us how at one time when people were making bread for an idol, each family member had his or her own task in preparing the bread: The children gathered wood, the father made the fire for the oven, and the mother made dough into bread (Jer. 7:18). This helps us imagine how families must have worked together in other ways as well.

Like the shepherdess in our little story in the chapter about Water, we know that boys and girls also tended their family's flock of sheep and goats, as did David (1 Sam. 16:11), Joseph (Gen. 37:2), Rachel (Gen. 29:9) and Zipporah and her sisters (Ex. 2:16). In countries where nomads live, children still do this work. (Nomads are people, usually shepherds, who live in tents.)

Children who were shepherds or shepherdesses worked very hard and had a lot of responsibility. Imagine walking every day several miles from your home to a place where you had to make sure all the sheep and goats had enough plants to nibble and a spring of water nearby. Not to mention making sure that none of them got lost. You also had to be very brave, because you might have to fight wild animals who wanted to eat your sheep, as we learned about young David (1 Sam 17:34-35 NCV).

Only your littlest brothers or sisters wouldn't have had some kind of work to do, as long as

Mosaic showing a man in his vineyard playing the flute, found in Beersheba (Gen. 21:14) (IAA)

they were too young to know how to do a job. When Solomon first became king of the Israelites, he prayed to God to help him because he felt he was like "a little child" who did not know how to carry out his duties (1 Kings 3:7).

When Lucian went off with his uncle to learn how to be a stone-worker, he became what is called an "apprentice." Historians tell us exactly how long children would spend as apprentices for some professions: It would take about a year to become a nail-maker or to learn how to play the flute. Apprenticing to become a weaver took four years, and for builders it was about six years. Apprentice slave children (about whom you'll read more below) had to work from sunup to sundown, but apprentices like Lucian were given holidays off.

A stable boy cleans a horse's hooves on this fourth-century AD Greek coin (Courtesy Numismatica Ars Classica, Auction 54, Lot 683)

Sometimes you had to leave your home and go to live in another place to be an apprentice. But most boys learned their father's trade, like Jesus did, probably working with Joseph (Matt. 13:55) every day. Some children were adopted by other families if that meant they had a chance to learn a profession; this practice went all the way back to the Laws of Hammurabi. (He was a Babylonian king who lived about 4,800 years ago and wrote one of the world's first lists of laws.)

Clay figurine of a woman kneading bread, from Old Testament times, Achziv (Josh. 15:44) (IAA)

In Bible days, many families were not free to decide who to work for. These people, called slaves, did not get paid for their work, although they were given food, clothing and shelter. Slaves in homes usually lived better and longer lives than those who worked hard in factories or mines, or outdoors in the fields. You might have to be a slave if your people were captured in a war. The Bible had rules about how people should treat their slaves, and encouraged people to set slaves free (Deut.15:12-15).

Do you know who the most famous slave girl in the Bible was? It was Miriam, who grew up to be a leader of her people (Mic. 6:4). Miriam saved the life of her baby brother, Moses, after their mother had to set him afloat in a basket on the Nile River to hide him from the Egyptians.

Around the time of Jesus, a father might free one of his slaves, and then allow that man to marry his daughter. Children whose parents were slaves in someone's home could grow up to manage the household, or have other important tasks. But even if a slave grew up in the master's household, got an education and had a good job – and even if he could marry the master's daughter – slaves and free people were never the same, according to Paul the Apostle, because only a son could receive his father's wealth after the father passed away (Gal. 4:4-7).

Statuette of a girl holding a pot for eye makeup (kohl), made of steatite, Egypt 1963-1787 BC (British Museum, London)

Slave boys or girls sometimes played interesting parts in Bible stories. Once when David was hiding from King Saul (who was very angry with him), Jonathan, Saul's son and David's best friend, said he would get a secret message to David. He told David to hide behind a rock in the field, where he could hear Jonathan but could not be seen, and Jonathan would shoot arrows toward the rock. David would know whether Saul was still angry with him according to which side of the rock the arrows landed on. Jonathan had a little boy with him, probably his slave, to pick up the arrows he shot. After "telling" David in this way Jonathan had to run away, Jonathan gave his bow and arrows to the boy and told him to take them back to town (1 Sam. 20:40). This was so the boy wouldn't see David come out, and then go and tell King Saul about David's friendship with the king's son, Jonathan.

In another story, a slave girl in the Bible was given an important, secret job. After David became king and his son Absalom rose up to fight against him, this young girl was supposed to get a message to David's friends Jonathan and Ahimaaz, telling them to hide from Absalom (2 Sam. 17:17-18).

One of the Ten Commandments made sure that everyone – even children – had time to rest each week. The Fourth Commandment forbids work on the Sabbath not only for the person in charge of the household, but for everyone in it – including those who did not have their own rights in those days, such as children, slaves, homeless people and even working animals (Ex. 20:10).

Activities

Be a good shepherd and lead the lost sheep on the left through the maze to its friends in the pen!

In the right-hand column, make a list of 10 duties you have at home. Are there any duties you have that children in Bible times also did? If you find any, draw a line connecting them.

Some Children's Duties in Bible Times	My Duties at Home
Taking the flock to pasture	
Emptying the chamber pot	
Cleaning the bedroom	
Making the bed	
Practicing music	
Gathering wood	
Fighting wild animals	
Bible lessons	
Working in the field	
Weaving	

Here is a picture of Miriam finding her baby brother Moses in the Nile River. The work tools you see on the left are hidden somewhere in the picture. Color them in when you find them.

Chapter 4
Animals

David's Wild Ride

David listened as hard as he could, in that special way of his, just as he did every night before he fell asleep. All he could hear was the soft shuffling and snorting of the nearby goats and sheep as they settled down for the night. That was a good thing. David was only 12 years old, but he had already been a shepherd for half his life, and now his father trusted him to lead the flock into the wilderness east of his home in Bethlehem. David knew that if any of the fearsome wild animals of the desert came close, the little herd would begin to move restlessly. If he thought a lion or a bear might be nearby, he would slip his slingshot out of his belt and creep even closer to the little corral he had built out of dry brush. When he saw the wild animal's eyes gleaming in the moonlight, David would wind up his slingshot and *whoo-o-osh* ... let loose the stone to find its target.

David then walked to the small hill where he could have a good view and wrapped himself in his cloak. He was very tired after a hard day keeping the animals together as they grazed and his eyelids quickly began to close. Suddenly the hill, which a moment ago seemed like any other barren wilderness hill, began to rise up, up, up to the night sky. And David rose up with it! The hill shook and shuddered and made a strange noise – it was the sound of an animal.

David turned to look behind him, and in front of him, and was amazed to find he was actually sitting on top of a huge oryx, or, as some people call them, a "wild ox of the desert." David had only seen these beautiful creatures from far away when they came to drink from the spring after he had led his flocks away from it. Now the sharp, straight horns of this tremendous animal were only inches from his face!

David turned to God: "Dear God, help me get me down from the back of this wild creature and I promise that when I grow up, I will build you a great, high temple!" Then, something amazing happened: David saw that God had called a lion out of nowhere. Although the oryx was so much bigger than the lion that it could have just stomped on it, it was very afraid of the great king of the beasts.

The oryx suddenly sank down to the ground, and David climbed off. But then a shiver raced down his spine as he realized he was now face to face with the lion! And so God sent a gazelle that ran between David and the lion. The lion ran off after the gazelle into the night, leaving David safe and sound with his sleeping flock.

Later, David wrote a special song of thanksgiving to God for saving him and asking God to always protect him from danger: "Rescue me from the lion's mouth and from the horns of these wild oxen" (Ps. 22:21 NIV).

This story comes from a legend in an ancient collection called the Midrash and from the words of Ps. 22:21 and 92:10.

Animal Talk

"But David said to Saul, 'I, your servant, have been keeping my father's sheep. When a lion or bear came and took a sheep from the flock, I would chase it. I would attack it and save the sheep from its mouth'" (1 Sam. 17:34-35 NCV)

In the first book of the Bible, Genesis, we see that God cares for all animals, because He commands Noah to bring a male and a female of each kind of animal into the ark to save them from the great flood He sent. Even the tiniest birds, like sparrows, are important: "...not one of them is forgotten in the sight of God" (Luke 12:6 NIV).

The Bible also uses what we know about animals to help us understand God's word. For example, Isaiah helps us picture the time of the Messiah by saying animals no longer fight and we can all live together, even with frightening ones: "Then wolves will live in peace with lambs, and leopards will lie down to rest with goats. Calves, lions, and young bulls will eat together, and a little child will lead them..." (Isa. 11:6-7 NCV).

Not every young boy or girl in Bible days met up with lions and bears like David did. But if you lived in those days, especially in the countryside, animals would be part of your everyday life. By the time of Jesus, people knew how to raise chickens in the Holy Land and little girls would learn how to feed and care for them by watching their mothers do it. Their job was to make sure that the mother hens sat on their eggs so they would hatch and the little chicks would come out strong. The sheep and goats herded by young boys and girls were very important to the family, giving them wool to weave into clothing, milk, and sometimes meat to eat. Their droppings would be used to make fires and as fertilizer to make their soil better.

Be Kind to Animals

If you lived in Bible days, your parents and teachers would have raised you to take good care of animals. The Bible says this makes you a good person (Prov. 12:10). In the story of the donkey that talked to its owner, Balaam, ancient wise men said God was angry with Balaam for beating his donkey. God said no one – neither people nor animals – should work on the Sabbath (Deut. 5:14). In fact, it was taught that you should feed your animal before you eat, because according to Deut. 11:15 (NCV), that is the order in which God sees to food for all creatures: "He will put grass in the fields for your cattle, and you will have plenty to eat."

The Bible offers other good rules for dealing with animals: Don't yoke an ox and a donkey together to your plow (Deut. 22:10) because it would be hard for the donkey

A small clay goose from Old Testament times, found at Qitmit in the Negev (IAA)

Crows in the desert

An oryx

A little clay cow from Old Testament times, found at H. Qitmit (Josh. 15:44) (IAA)

to keep up with the ox, which is stronger. When an ox (Deut. 25:4) or perhaps your donkey, was helping you thresh your grain – which means separating the seeds from the stalks – you were not allowed to put anything over its mouth to keep it from eating fallen grain if it got hungry. When people hunted birds for food, they were not allowed to take a mother bird together with its chicks or its eggs (Deut. 22:6-7), because it would make the mother feel sad.

Pets

Just like today, people kept pets of all kinds. One picture on a vase made by the ancient Greeks shows a little girl holding a turtle on a leash; an ancient sculpture shows children with pet birds. Some people raised monkeys, cats, mongooses, birds, squirrels, and even sea lions. But the Bible never has a good word to say about dogs. One verse in Psalms pictured wild dogs surrounding and attacking people (Ps. 22:16). The Bible also tells us that dogs lived in the city dump (1 Kings 21:23). Still, we know people did have dogs inside their homes, because the Gospels mention dogs waiting for food to fall from the table (Matt.15:27, Mark 7:28). People kept cats to catch mice and snakes.

King Solomon's sailors brought both monkeys and apes from India to the Holy Land (1 Kings 10: 21-23). In later times monkeys were trained to serve food, pour water over peoples' hands before they ate, and even to clean house.

In Jesus' day, you might try to scurry out of the way if you saw a horse ridden by a Roman soldier. Horses were used mainly by soldiers, which is why Proverbs 21:31 (NLT) says: "The horse is prepared for the day of battle..." But in a big Roman city in the Holy Land – like Caesarea (Acts 8:40; Acts 24-25) – you might have gone with your parents to the stadium to see a chariot race. By the time of Emperor Augustus, during whose reign Jesus was born, there were four racing teams, named after colors: the white, the red, the blue and the green. People rooted for them just as loudly as you might do today for your favorite sports team.

A panther head, perhaps part of a piece
of stone furniture
(Gabi Laron, courtesy Yotam Tepper and Orit Peleg-
Barkat, Ramat Hanadiv Excavation, Hebrew University)

Wild Animals

If you lived in a small village or close to the desert, you might come across various wild and dangerous animals, such as wolves or hyenas. To avoid the animals that would be out at night, some dinner guests would make sure to eat early and go home during the daylight hours.

One desert animal was the oryx – like the one in our story that David went riding on – which is a member of the antelope family. The English Bible calls the oryx a "wild ox" (Job 39:9, Numbers 23:22). Today, you can see this beautiful creature and many other wild animals in a special preserve in southern Israel called Hai-Bar Yotvata. Its long, straight horns line up so perfectly that from the side, it looks like it has only one horn. So when travelers first saw the oryx, they told people back home they had seen a creature called a unicorn (which means "one horn"). Some say that is how the legend of the unicorn was born.

There were almost no oryx left in the Holy Land until nature-lovers began helping them to survive. Some animals that once lived in the Holy Land, like lions (Judges 14:5, 1 Chron. 11:22) and bears (1 Sam. 17:34; 2 Sam 17:8), can no longer be found there. The bears that once lived in the Holy Land, called Syrian bears, were smaller than the American grizzly. People saw the last wild bear in the Holy Land more than 100 years ago near Mount Tabor. But you might still see foxes (Neh. 4:3, Luke 9:58) and wolves (Gen. 49:27, John 10:12) living in the wild, even today.

Many people in Bible days were named after animals, like Jael, Deborah, Rachel, Zipporah, Jonah, Shaphan and Caleb. Do you know who these people are and what their names mean? Turn to the Activities section on the next page to find out.

Talking to the Animals

The Bible teaches that wise King Solomon "taught about animals, birds, reptiles and fish" (1 Kings 4:33 NIV), and so people believed he also knew how to talk to animals. The most famous talking animal in the Bible (besides the snake in the story of Adam and Eve) belonged to a magician of a people called the Moabites, whose name was Balaam.

The Moabite king Balak did not want the Israelites to enter the Promised Land, so he asked Balaam to put a curse on them. But while Balaam was riding his donkey on his way to curse the Israelites, the donkey saw an angel and stopped in its tracks. Balaam beat the donkey, but it refused to budge. The Bible says: "Then the Lord made the donkey talk, and she said to Balaam, 'What have I done to make you hit me three times?' Balaam answered the donkey, 'You have made me look foolish!'... But the donkey said to Balaam, 'I am your very own donkey, which you have ridden for years. Have I ever done this to you before?' 'No,' Balaam said. Then the Lord let Balaam see the angel of the Lord... The angel of the Lord asked Balaam, 'Why have you hit your donkey three times? I have stood here to stop you, because what you are doing is wrong. The donkey saw me and turned away from me three times. If she had not turned away, I would have killed you by now, but I would have let her live'" (Numbers 22:28-33, NCV).

Ancient wise men taught is that the talking donkey shows us what kind of a person Balaam really was: He had wanted to hurt Israel by using the words of a curse, he could not even control his own donkey, and even a donkey could see the angel of the Lord, but Balaam could not.

Meanwhile, the Crocodile

The crocodile is mentioned many times in the Bible, as a sea monster (Isa. 51:9, Job 7:12). Ezekiel says that crocs are strong animals, but that God is always stronger. The

A mosaic lion, from Hamat Tiberias (John 6:23) (IAA)

Stamp with the name "Gmaryahu son of Shaphan" (Jer. 36:10) from Old Testament times, found in the City of David. *Shaphan* in Hebrew is a small animal called a hyrax (see page 41) (IAA)

Camel resting by the walls of Jerusalem

A bird is one of the many pictures in this mosaic, which decorated the floor of the ancient synagogue at Ein Gedi

39

Bible tells us that when Aaron threw down his staff before the Pharaoh, it became a "snake" (Ex. 7:10) – a *tannin*, which is the Hebrew word for crocodile. So Aaron was showing Pharaoh that God was stronger than even the strongest animal in the Nile River. In Israel, you can take a nature walk along Crocodile Stream, which comes down from Mount Carmel and had crocodiles in it many hundreds of years ago.

The Bible teaches us that all of God's creatures are amazing in their own way. That is why the sages of old taught that when people see an unusual animal, they should say a special blessing, which you might like to learn. It goes like this: "Blessed are you God, King of the World, who has created so many different kinds of creatures."

Coin showing Agrippa II (Acts 25:13) as a boy, riding a horse
(Drawn by Pnina Arad; courtesy of Pnina Arad)

Activities

Who Am I?

1. When I get angry, I spit! I was used to carry heavy loads in ancient caravans, and that's why I'm often called the "ship of the desert." Job owned 3,000 animals like me (Job 1:3).

2. My horns are very straight, long and thin. In the Bible, I'm called an "ox" (Ps. 92:10).

3. I'm a hunter that used to live wild in the deserts of Israel. Jeremiah the Prophet said I could not change my spots (Jer. 13:23).

4. People have used me to carry themselves and their belongings from Bible times to this day. In the Bible, one of my species could talk to his owner (Num. 22:28-33).

5. I look a little bit like a fox and a little bit like a dog. I live in the desert and I'm known for howling (Mic. 1:8 NIV), especially at night. And I'll eat almost anything.

6. People say I'm a tricky animal. Jesus called Antipas, who wanted to kill him, by my name (Luke 13:32).

You'll find the answers on page 144

Biblical People Named after Animals

The following biblical people were named after animals. Look up their stories and try to think of good things about each animal that would lead the parents to name their child after it. You might also be able to think of some ways in which some of these people acted like the animals they were named after.

Jael (Judges 4:17-22; Judges 5:24): ibex or mountain goat

Deborah the judge (Judges 4:4-4:9; 5:7): bee

Rachel (Gen. 29:6-30:8): lamb

Zipporah (Ex. 2:21-22; Ex. 18:2): bird

Jonah (Book of Jonah, Luke 11:30): dove

Shaphan (2 Kings 22:3; 22:10-14): coney, also called hyrax or "rock badger." (Ps. 104:18 and Prov. 30:26 will tell you something about this animal.)

Chapter 5
Toys and Games

The Lost-and-Found Doll

Martha's grandmother had a twinkle in her eye this morning, because this was the day her granddaughter had been awaiting for many weeks. Every day the 8-year-old girl had been watching impatiently at the loom for the moment her grandmother would leave her weaving and pick up the doll she was making for Martha out of small pieces of unused cloth or thread.

Martha often spent her mornings next to Grandma at the loom and would point out pieces of lambs' wool that had not yet been made into thread that could be used for stuffing, bits of blue and red cloth that became a tunic, and a little woven red wool for a mantle. The doll's arms and legs were made of the fine linen her father had fondly handed to Martha as soon as she asked. The linen came from the piles of material ready for market that he bought from the linen makers who had made her city, Scythopolis, the most famous in the **Decapolis**.

Grandma had already sewn some black goat hair thread to the doll's head, making a pretty hairdo. This morning it was time for the finishing touches: Grandma took two small blue glass beads from her own necklace and sewed them to the doll's hair, and it was done.

At that moment, her father appeared in the doorway, ready for the walk to the market. "Run and get your cloak, Martha," he said, and she returned with it in a flash. Papa usually did not take the children into the city markets, so this was a special day. True, they could see amazing sights – people and even wild animals from faraway countries. But the streets were crowded and sometimes even dangerous, and little girls whose families had servants to do their shopping were not supposed to be out and about.

As they walked, Martha whispered to her new doll about all the colorful places they passed. The townspeople bowed their heads in greeting to her father. He was a leader in their congregation. When he was not busy buying and selling linen, he would spend hours with the Christian monks in the monastery on the outskirts of town. The monks had taught Martha's papa many stories from the Holy Scriptures, including

one about King Saul, who died after a battle with the Philistines near their city, back when it was called Beit Shean.

They had just stepped down from the covered market into the street itself. Suddenly Martha heard people shouting: "Make way! Make way!" She looked down the street but, of course, could see nothing but the legs of people and animals, and the wheels of the many carts. Just in time, her father scooped her up into his arms and moved quickly back onto the sidewalk, out of path of an oncoming caravan of camels heading for the spice market.

Martha could not take her eyes off the endless line of camels as they lumbered past with their burdens of straw baskets and woolen bags swaying from their humps. She had to stretch her neck to look at their funny, long faces. Finally, the caravan ended and they crossed the street. Her father put her down, and they began walking again.

But wait, where was her little doll? She let out a loud wail and tears came rolling down her cheeks. "Are you hurt, my child?" her father asked her, feeling her arms and legs to see if she had been struck by a camel's foot or a swinging basket. She could hardly get the words out between sobs. "No-o-o-o, I...can't...find...Mary!"

"Who is Mary?" her father asked. Papa did not know that Martha had given it the best name she knew as soon as Grandma placed it in her arms.

"My dol-l-l-l-l," Martha wailed.

Her father looked at her sorrowfully. What could he do? He helped her look around the street, to see if she had dropped it before the camels went by. No trace of her beautiful cloth Mary could be found.

The sun was getting higher in the sky and the bales of linen should not wait if they were to cross the Jordan River before sunset, so her father said: "Never mind, we'll explain to Grandma and have her make you another Mary."

When they got to the linen-sellers' market, she watched as her father ordered the loading of the cloth into its wagons. But she was trying to imagine what had happened to Mary, and she could only think that she had been trampled under the camels' large feet. She shut her eyes tight and tried not to think about that any more.

But when she got home, her grandma, being grandma, folded her in her warm arms, and comforted her. "Perhaps Mary went to live in a new, wonderful home," she said.

Little did she know! That Sunday, the family went off to the monastery outside the city to watch the beautiful service. Outside, as usual, sat beggars, sometimes whole families waiting for a coin or a piece of food. When her father stopped to give a coin to one family, Martha could not believe her eyes – a little girl just about her age, with matted hair and dark eyes peering out from the dirty face, was cradling her cloth doll Mary in her arms.

"Papa, Papa," Martha pulled at her father's cloak and pointed excitedly. "It's Mary," she whispered. "Please, get her back for me!"

But her father knelt down until his face was level with hers, and said: "Now is a time for you to remember that God taught us: 'you shall not harden your heart, nor close your hand to your poor brother; but you shall freely open your hand to him...' Moses taught us that from the word of God!* And John the Baptist said: "Anyone who has two shirts should share with the one who has none."**

45

"But Papa, it's not a shirt – it's Mary!" Martha protested.

"As soon as we get home, we'll ask grandma to start making you another doll. But this little girl has no grandmother who can sit in the courtyard, no loom to weave on, no scraps to make a doll out of. Think how happy Mary is now, to bring pleasure to a little girl who has nothing," Papa said.

Martha never forgot Mary, the little doll she lost that day in the city. And she never forgot her father's Scripture lesson either.

*(Deut. 15:7 NASB). **(Luke 3:11 NIV).

What does it mean?

Decapolis – This word means "ten cities" in Greek, and Scythopolis, the biblical Beit Shean, was one of them. The Gospels (Matt, 4:25; Mark 5:20; Mark 7:31) mention that Jesus visited these towns.

Marble statue of a young girl playing with knucklebones, about 1,800 years old, found in Rome. (Pergamon Museum, Berlin)

Toys and Games

"And the streets will be filled with boys and girls playing"
(Zech. 8:5 NCV)

The Bible does not often mention children playing and when it does, it's to teach us important lessons – not about games or toys, but about how we should behave or what the Bible has in store for us in the future. For example, in the verse that begins this chapter, the prophet Zechariah tells us about the wonderful future of Jerusalem by saying "the streets will be filled with boys and girls playing..." (Zech. 8:5).

But what games did children play? Were they anything like the games you play today? If the Bible doesn't mention the games or the toys, how can we know? To find that out, we have to look at ancient artifacts – items from olden times that are uncovered later by archaeologists.

And that brings us to another good question: What is a toy? What would you answer if someone asked you that? If you said "something I play with," then how do archaeologists know when they have found something children played with way back then? Sometimes they know because these objects (or pictures or carvings of them) were toys at other times in history; in fact, children play with some of these – like a yoyo or a top – until this very day. Sometimes we find pictures of ancient toys or sculptures of children playing games. Sometimes ancient writers talked about children playing games and how they played them.

As you'll see in this chapter, children played not only with specially made toys. In fact, almost anything can be a toy – even sticks and stones like ones you've probably played with. Can you picture yourself playing with a little mouse you found outside? Ancient Roman children did just that, according to a poet named Horace, who says he knew of children who made a little cart and hitched it to a mouse, pretending the mouse was a horse. And as we mentioned in the chapter on Animals, a picture on a Greek vase shows a little girl playing with a turtle on a leash.

As for dolls, archaeologists have found dolls like the one Martha lost in our story in this chapter, and there are also pictures and sculptures of girls playing with dolls.

Babies in Bible times, just like today, often received a rattle for their first toy. The rattles were made of clay and filled with seeds to make a sound when shaken. Usually painted with bright colors, the rattles were sometimes shaped like animals. There were also whistles made of pottery, sometimes in animal shapes.

(Shutterstock)

Flute made out of an animal bone, about 2,200 years old, found in the City of David (IAA)

Pull-toy, Roman period, found in central Israel (IAA)

Children have always loved to play. In fact, one Greek word for child, *pais*, comes from a word meaning "play." But because in the old days (and in some parts of the world even now), kids sometimes had to be ready when they were very young help their families earn a living and they had very little time to play with their toys. In Greek and Roman days, when the moment came for a girl to get married and she would no longer have time to play with her toys, there would be a special ceremony when she put away all the dolls she played with when she was little. And that's what Paul the Apostle meant when he said: "...when I became a man, I put away childish things" (1 Cor. 13:11).

Ruins of the ancient city of Beit Shean, where our little story takes place

One game children played in New Testament times was hoop-rolling, where a large hoop was rolled along the ground with the help of a stick – the idea was to keep the hoop rolling along for as long as possible. A Roman poet named Martial, who lived during the first century AD, writes about hoops "with tinkling rings" that boys played with. Adults also played hoop-and-stick, for exercise.

Speaking of exercise, children in the Holy Land today are lucky when it comes to playing outside, because it doesn't rain all summer long. One thing we know children in the ancient Holy Land did together for fun was to pick flowers – one story from those days tells us about two children picking flowers who wandered into a cemetery by accident!

Modern statue of a girl playing with a hoop, a game enjoyed by ancient kids, too
(Courtesy of Kent Wade)

Pretending to Do What Grown-ups Do

Kids can make a toy out of almost anything, including grown-up stuff. In the chapter on Milestones in Life, you'll learn that when Moses was a little boy he took the Pharaoh's crown and put it on his own head. He probably thought it was a fun thing to do, but the adults were afraid it meant Moses was going to become the king instead of Pharaoh.

In Roman times, children played pretend – they liked to imagine they were kings, gladiators and athletes, and anyone who was a hero to them. When they played soldier, they sometimes wore a little "helmet" out of straw that had ornaments hanging from it. An ancient Greek writer named Epictetus says children even imitated tax collectors. It's hard to imagine a child in Jesus' day wanting to "play tax collector" unless he was a bully – the New Testament tells us that collectors were considered mean and greedy (although one of them, Levi, who collected taxes in Capernaum, became one of Jesus' followers (Mark 2:14; Luke 5:27.)

Ivory Egyptian game board, around 1,200–1,400 years old, found at Megiddo
(IAA)

An ancient Jewish source from around the time of Jesus describes how children could have fun while their mothers, grandmothers and big sisters were baking bread – they would be given a little piece of dough with which they could make their own play bread or form it into interesting shapes like kids today do with modeling clay.

Rabbi Gamaliel (Paul's teacher) was in Rome when he saw children making piles of fruit, pointing to each pile and saying they were for different kinds of gifts to give the Temple in Jerusalem, as the Bible says to do (Numbers 18:25-31; Deut. 12:11).

Game board made of chalk stone, around 4,000 years old, found at Arad (IAA)

When Jesus wanted to tell people that they did not listen to his teachings, but were arguing over unimportant things, he said they were like "children sitting in the marketplace, who call out to each other: 'We played music for you, but you did not dance; we sang a sad song, but you did not cry'" (Matt. 11:16-17; Luke 7:31-33 NCV). Jesus might have pointed to children right there in the market, trying to decide which kind of game to play – a happy game of pretending they were at a wedding where flutes were played, or a slow game of singing a sad song called a dirge, like people did at funerals.

Did you ever play the game where you hide something in one of your hands behind your back, then bring your hands around front and ask your friends to pick the hand with the hidden object? Well, in ancient Greece, that game was called *posinda*. An ancient historian and soldier called Xenophon said the game was good practice for learning how to be a smart soldier during a battle.

Knucklebones – "Dice" in Bible Days

The bones people used in this game were not peoples' knuckles! They were the small bones from the ankles of sheep or goats. In Greek, these bones were called *astragali*. Each side of the bone looked different, so each could stand for a different number. Depending on which side the bone landed after they threw it in the air, they could win points they could add up.

An ancient animal knucklebone (IAA)

In a different knucklebone game, players threw the bones up in the air and saw how many they could catch on the back of one hand, like one of the ways of playing jacks. Mostly girls are shown playing this game. The girl you see in the ancient sculpture on page 46 is playing quietly. But in one sculpture made in Rome in the first century BC, a boy is shown biting the leg of another boy, with the knucklebone-game pieces scattered in front of him. What a sore loser!

Dolls

Children have been playing with dolls for thousands of years. Archaeologists found some dolls in Corinth, Greece from about 500 years before the birth of Jesus, and in Egypt from even before that. Dolls are shown on gravestones or found in girls' graves, so we know quite a bit about what the dolls looked like. Archaeologists have uncovered ancient dolls, made of clay, bone, wood and ivory, as well as rag dolls like the one in the picture at right, and the one little Martha lost in the story that begins this chapter.

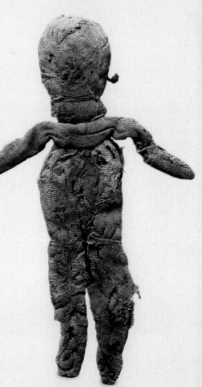

Rag doll, made of wool, papyrus, linen and glass, 1,500–1,900 years old, found in Oxyrhynchus, Egypt. She inspired the doll in the little story in this chapter
(British Museum, London)

Dolls also had miniature pieces of furniture and household things (for example, a tiny ladle and cup, a footstool and a dish). There were also small dollhouses, which the Roman poet Horace called "baby-houses."

49

Small clay statue of a cat, about 3,000 years old, found at Achziv on the shore of northern Israel
(IAA)

It seems most dolls depicted girls (the word for doll in Latin is *pupa*, which also means "little girl"). But we can imagine a boy playing with an "action doll," like the little gladiator dating from the first century AD that was found in Pergamon, an ancient Greek city.

Playing in the Water

How do we know children played in the water? One hint comes from Ps. 104:26, which gives praise to God for feeding all the animals in the sea. In that Psalm, it says God made the Leviathan (perhaps a whale) "to play in the sea" – as if the whale was one of God's children and God was watching it play.

An early Christian legend says that when Jesus was a boy, he went out to play near his house after a rainstorm and found water running down in little streams, so he made small pools out of them by blocking them off with mud.

It's easy to picture children by a stream in Jesus' time or back in the earliest days of the Bible, because when their mothers went to get water to use at home – which they did every day in the morning and the evening – they would have taken their younger children with them. One ancient Jewish source tells about children playing outside in water, dunking each other. Ancient writers talk about both boys and girls playing by the water. Girls are described by the seashore making sandcastles and drawing figures in the sand.

Animal Toys

Clay rattle, about 3,000 years old, found at Hazor in northern Israel
(IAA)

Some of the small clay figures of animals that have been found in excavations might have been toys for children. The story above about Jesus playing by the stream also says he made 12 little sparrows out of clay. One ancient source mentions a wooden horse. In Egypt, children played with clay animals including sheep and birds, and also alligators, – which lived in the Nile, the great river of Egypt. Animal statues were usually very real-looking, sometimes even scary, like a bear with its mouth open as if it was roaring. But sometimes there were funny animals too, like a bird with antlers.

Nutty Fun

Walnuts
(Shutterstock)

Children did not often eat at the table with adults, but there was at least one meal each year where children were supposed to be present – that was the special springtime holiday meal of Passover, where the father of the family would tell the story of how the Israelites escaped from Egyptian slavery (Ex. 12: 14; Deut. 16:1; Matt. 26:18; Luke 2:41). That special meal called the Seder is still celebrated by Jews all over the world. At the Seder meal, children were given nuts and toasted pieces of grain either to play games with (like "guess how many are in my hand") or to eat – or both – to keep them awake and interested. To this day, games and fun songs are part of the Passover meal. By the way, it's the job of the youngest child at the table to ask four special questions. In answering them, the father or leader of the Seder tells the whole story of the Israelites' escape from Egypt.

We also read about children who hollowed out a pomegranate or a nut to make into scales when they played "market" (another example of playing "real-life" games like we mentioned above.) One tombstone from Italy about from the second century AD shows

13 children, boys and girls, playing a game with nuts. A stone coffin is decorated with a carving of boys playing with a pile of nuts. It looks like a boy is waiting his turn to try and roll down one nut that will get the whole pile to fall apart.

Play Ball!

Ball games were popular in the ancient world, both with children and adults. Children in ancient Greece tried to see if they could catch a ball with their eyes closed; they also juggled and played stickball. Ancient balls made of cloth on a frame of reeds have been found in Greece and Egypt. The Roman poet Martial mentions a ball that was filled inside with feathers. The Christian writer Jerome said parents could give their daughters "pretty balls" if they finished their chores on time.

Costumed youngsters enjoying a circle game
(Nazareth Village)

We also know people in Jesus' time played ball, because Jewish wise men from around that time used a ball game to help people understand the meaning of one of the verses of the Bible. That verse is in the Book of Ecclesiastes 12:11 (NCV), where it says that the words of wise men are like "teachings that come from one Shepherd." They wanted people to understand that the wise words that guided people how to live came from God and were passed on from parents to children and teachers to students like a ball being passed from hand to hand by girls at play.

Play Nice...

Sometimes the Bible tells us how we should live and behave by telling us stories about bad behavior. One example of this is a way that "youths" played by making fun of an adult, in this case – Elisha the prophet, whom they teased and called "baldhead" (2 Kings 2:23). According to the Bible, bears came out of the woods and attacked these youths. Not far from the place where this happened, north of Jerusalem, is a village called Deir Dubwan, whose name means "the monastery of the bears." No one knows exactly how it got this name, but perhaps people remembered that scary story and built a monastery where they thought it happened.

The Bible also tells the story about a boy – Ishmael – who was not very nice to his brother Isaac. The two brothers, Isaac and Ishmael, were the sons of Abraham the Patriarch. Isaac's mother was Sarah, and Ishmael's mother was Hagar, who was Sarah's servant. One day Sarah saw Ishmael, who was older than Isaac, "making fun of Isaac" (Gen. 21:9 NCV). She became very angry and told Abraham he had to send Hagar and Ishmael away, which he did.

Biblical Board Games: For Grownups Only?

Archaeologists tell us that people have been playing "board games" for at least 8,000 years and that they were played by grownups, not kids! Sometimes people carved them out of stone right on the street so, for example, a storeowner could play while waiting for customers. Even soldiers on guard duty played them. One ancient game people still play is called Mankala. The "game board," carved in stone or in the sand, was made of two rows of little pits and the players try to push pebbles, shells or seeds from one hole to another. Archaeologists have found this game in excavations in the Holy Land, including Tiberias and Beit Shean.

Activities

The Walnut Game

Instructions
1. Make a pyramid-shaped pile of 20 walnuts in their shells.
2. Draw a chalk circle around the pile if you're playing on a sidewalk. If you're playing in a yard, you can make a circle in the dirt.
3. Give each player three walnuts. (You can get ready for this game by having each player decorate their walnuts with paints or magic markers so everyone knows which ones are theirs!)
4. Stand at least five feet from the pile.
5. Each player throws a walnut at the pile and tries to knock as many walnuts out of the circle as possible.
6. When the pile is gone, but there are still walnuts in the circle, players take aim at the nuts that are left and try to knock them out of the circle.
7. The walnuts you knock out of the circle are yours. The player with the most walnuts when the circle is empty wins.

The Pit Game

An outdoor game
1. Save your apricot pits to use in this game. (They're the easiest to clean after you've eaten the fruit, but you can use peach pits, too.)
2. Dig a little hole in the ground next to a wall or fence.
3. Give each player 10 pits.
4. Players stand or kneel at least five feet from the hole.
5. Throw your pits one by one into the hole; you can aim straight at the hole or aim at the wall/fence right above the hole. Keep throwing until you miss. Then it's the next player's turn.
6. The player that runs out of pits first wins.

Twenty Squares – A Game for Two Players

1. Draw a game board on cardboard, copying the lines as you see them in the ancient Canaanite game board below. There will be a total of 20 squares. At one end will be four rows of three squares each. The middle row will have eight squares, from one end to the other. In the row of eight, draw an X the fourth, eighth, and twelfth squares.
2. Make your own dice: you can find a roughly cube-shaped pebble and write a number on each side: 1, 2, 3, 4. Or, you can make dice out of modeling clay or regular clay, make a real cube and decorate it.
3. Place the game board lengthwise between you. Roll your dice to see who goes first (the person with the highest number).
4. The first player rolls the dice and advances the number of spaces indicated by the dice. If you "leap over" the other player's playing piece, you send them back to the starting point. But if you land on an X, you're "safe" from being sent back to the start. Move your pieces back and forth across the short rows. When you land on the middle box of the last short row, you're ready to move up the long row to the finish.
5. The winner of the game is the player who is able to move all of his or her pieces safely down to the X at the end of the long row.

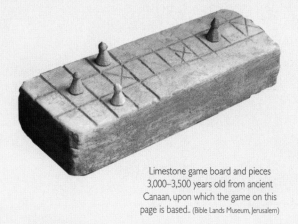

Limestone game board and pieces 3,000–3,500 years old from ancient Canaan, upon which the game on this page is based.. (Bible Lands Museum, Jerusalem)

Bone die (a pair of these is called dice), about 3,000 years old, found in the City of David, Jerusalem. (IAA)

Chapter 6
Milestones in Life

Be a Myrtle, not a Thorn!

Joshua knew that something important was about to happen. He was crouching in the courtyard by the doorway to their one-room home as the sun began to set behind the mountains on the far shore of the Sea of Galilee. The grown-ups walked by without noticing he was there.

His father, Yosei, his two uncles and their wives had all stepped over the high stone threshold into the room. His two older brothers were also there. When each of them turned 18, they had married and got fishing boats of their own, joining their father in his boat as they set sail every day on the Sea of Galilee.

What would they decide? Nervously, he fingered the little bags of herbs and spices sewn into the edges of his shirt. At age 12, he felt like he was too old to be wearing these little pouches. All the mothers in Capernaum sewed them onto their children's shirts, believing it protected them from illness. These things are for babies, he protested every time his mother put fresh herbs, salt and pollen in the little bags and threw away the old ones.

But if things inside went his way, he would soon be able to do much more than wear grown-up clothing. If they went to Jerusalem, he would receive the blessing of the elders in the Temple. Then he would be on his way to being a man.

After that, if Joshua worked hard enough at his swimming lessons with his father and could manage the dangerous afternoon waves of the Sea of Galilee, he would be allowed to go fishing with his father and older brothers.

The grown-ups spoke in low murmurs because they did not want the neighbors to overhear them talking, which was easy to do because all of the houses were crowded very close together. If people heard what they said, the news would spread faster than it did when Joshua's little sister had been born, and all the village women had come immediately to celebrate.

The family felt it was not yet time for their neighbors to know that they would not be fulfilling the commandment to go to God's House with the offerings of some of their harvest. But none of their neighbors was any better off than they were, Joshua thought. This year the Roman tax collectors had taken even more of their profits than usual, and everyone was just trying to make sure their family had enough to eat.

What a difference between this year and last! After the wedding of Joshua's older sister last year, he and his brother Josiah had walked ahead of her, seated on a carriage piled high with woven blankets, a fine wooden bed-frame, cooking pots and oil lamps, dried beans and wheat from the last harvest, dates, fig-cakes and other sweets – all provided by their father. All their aunts and girl cousins had surrounded the cart, their eyes shining with happiness reflected in the light of their oil lamps.

But this year, the fish had refused to swim into his father's nets, no matter how many hours he and his brothers worked to mend them. And so, after feeding the family there were no tiny sardines left to salt and sell later. And still, the Roman soldiers, their armor clanking and the nails on the bottoms of their shoes echoing frighteningly on the cobbled street of the village, had taken much of the food people had stored in the large jars in the courtyard, as well as the dates drying on the roof.

He listened from the doorway. "Even if we had a good enough harvest to set aside some for our offerings, to pay for our journey to Jerusalem and to purchase a sacrifice – how would we pay our taxes to the king?" Joshua may not have had his blessing yet, but there was not a child in the village who didn't know that though the king sat far away in Jerusalem, his evil tax collectors were never far off.

That decided it. If they did not pay their taxes, they could lose their land and their boats to the local governor, who answered to the king. They would not go.

The adults ended their meeting and left the room. To his surprise, his father mussed up his hair lovingly and took him by the hand to the roof. Sitting under the lean-to, his father gestured to the place in front of him on the mat for Joshua to sit.

He thought he saw a bit of a twinkle in his father's tired eyes. "My son, soon enough you will be old enough to be in the room with us instead of hiding behind the door, when we make these decisions. I know you were looking forward to entering the Temple courts this year to be blessed by the elders. But sadly, we cannot go if we want to keep our land and feed the family with the little we have left after we pay our taxes."

Joshua decided that he would not let his father see his disappointment. Then came another surprise.

"I have not forgotten my promise to you last fall on Tabernacles – that your turn would come for your blessing by the elders. Our sages taught that it was a beautiful custom for this blessing to be given in Jerusalem. But who's to say we can't do it right here in our own village, in our own synagogue? I have spoken to your teachers, and they have agreed. They know you are a good student and a good son, studying hard, working hard and respectful of your elders," his father said.

"This Sabbath, after the reading of the Torah, they have agreed to bless you in the synagogue before all our neighbors and friends. What do you say?"

Joshua knew that in asking his opinion, he had already received a greater blessing than all the elders in Jerusalem could give him.

The Sabbath came, the community gathered. The elders were in their usual position in the front of the synagogue, close to the Holy Ark, where the Bible scrolls were kept. Joshua was called to the center of the room, where the Torah reading had just taken place. Their leader, the white-haired Rabbi Judah, was so old he could hardly rise from the Moses Seat near the synagogue doorway. Two of his grandsons helped him to the center of the room, holding two plants. "What in the world is this?" the people murmured to each other.

Rabbi Judah, his hand on Joshua's shoulder, spoke to the people. "Joshua son of Yosei had hoped, like we all did, to be able to go to Jerusalem this Passover. Who among us does not want to be blessed by giving our offerings in the place where God said His name will be? But for most of us, this Passover it is not to be. Let this child's longing be our own, and let us bless him for it."

Turning to Joshua, Rabbi Judah said: "I have before me a myrtle branch and a thorn. We know they both grow together in all of our fields. This is the challenge for you: Be like the myrtle branch, flowering and giving forth a good scent, and not like the thorn – dry and scratching at our feet in our fields. Continue your studies, be a good son to your father and your mother, and a servant of the Lord Almighty."

Joshua smelled the sweet aroma of the myrtle's leaves, and peeked up at the old man as he raised the branch and touched it to his brown curls. Then Rabbi Judah lay his hands over Joshua's head. He closed his wrinkled eyes for a moment, then raised them heavenward, saying: "In the presence of this congregation, may God bless this boy to his parents, his brothers and sisters, and raise him to a life of Torah and good deeds."

As Joshua walked with his family and the other villagers from the main room of the synagogue to the room where the women had set up a modest meal of celebration, he felt quite pleased with himself. And maybe next year – they would all go to Jerusalem.

Growing Up in Bible Days: Milestones in Children's Lives

"When I was a child, I spoke and thought and reasoned as a child. But when I grew up, I put away childish things"
(1 Cor.13:11 NLT)

A milestone is a marker that the ancient Romans used to place alongside roads to tell travelers how much farther they had to go until the next city, and other important information. You can still see some ancient Roman milestones in the Holy Land. But "milestone" has also come to mean an important point in people's lives, when they move from one stage of life to another.

In this chapter we will look at different stages in the lives of children of the Bible and try to understand how they are similar to, or different from, stages of life today. We will also look at what we can learn about people of all ages from the special ways the Bible teaches us about children.

An ancient Jewish teaching divided the stages of life into many smaller parts: At age 5, as we learned in the chapter on Education, you were ready to study Bible. At age 10, you were ready to learn the explanations of the Bible called the Mishnah. When you were 20 years old in Bible days, you were considered grown-up enough to give a half-shekel (a biblical coin) to the Tabernacle (Ex. 30:11-14) and later, to the Temple (Matt. 17:27).

As you got older, you were supposed learn more about life, becoming wise enough to be a leader in the community by the time you were 30. As people grew old, the saying about times in life teaches that age 80 was a time for "special strength." In fact, in Hebrew, age 80 is called *gvurot*, which means 'special strength.' According to the saying about stages in life, by age 70 people had gray hair, and age 100 was when God called them home. But since Moses lived until he was 120 (Deut. 34:7), to this day, as a special birthday blessing, people say: "May you live to 120!"

Scripture tells us that God was with Ishmael (Gen. 21:20) and Samuel (1 Sam. 3:19) as they grew up. Luke talks about Jesus growing up in this way: "...the child grew up and became strong. He was filled with wisdom, and God's goodness was on him" (Luke 2:40 NCV).

Back in the early days of the Bible, however, there were hardly any laws to protect children like there are today. In those days, for example, a father could even sell his daughter into slavery (Ex. 21:7). But by around the time

A statue of Mary and Elizabeth, the mother of John the Baptist, in a church in Ein Karem, where Elizabeth lived (Luke 1:26-40) (Courtesy of Miriam Feinberg Vamosh)

These doors at the Church of the Annunciation in Nazareth (where the Angel Gabriel told Mary she would give birth to Jesus) show the milestones in Jesus' life. On the left, top to bottom: Jesus' birth; going to Egypt; growing up in Nazareth. On the right, bottom to top: Jesus' baptism; Jesus preaching in Galilee; the crucifixion and resurrection (Courtesy of Eva Marie Everson)

of Jesus, Jewish people started making rules about protecting children, based on the Bible. For example, as we learned in the chapter on Work, sometimes a child had to sell vegetables in the market to help his family make a living. But the Jewish sages decided that children could not sell land or houses, because they did not have enough experience in life to do that and might make a mistake.

Mark tells us that one day, Jesus took a little child in his arms and said to the people: "Anyone who welcomes a little child like this on my behalf welcomes me..." (Mark 9:37 NLT). Jesus was telling people they had to take good care of their children.

Paul the Apostle taught that children weren't perfect and had lots to learn (1 Cor. 13:9-11). But Paul, like other Jews and Christians (and unlike many other people in ancient times), believed children knew things even grown-ups did not know, saying that God had "hidden these things from the people who are wise and smart. But you have shown them to those who are like little children" (Matt. 11:25-26 NCV). That was why Jesus said that in some ways people need to "change and become like little children" (Matt. 18:3 NCV).

Sometimes, as we'll see in the Bible stories below, children said and did things that grown-ups could not because God blesses the young in special ways.

A Baby Is Born

The most famous story in the Bible about a birth is, of course, the birth of Jesus in Bethlehem. Even though Mary had to give birth in a barn, because there was no room for the family anywhere else, she probably had women there to help her. Women who help mothers give birth are called "midwives" and are mentioned in the Bible. The midwives in Egypt saved the Israelite boys when Pharaoh was going to kill them, and that's how Moses survived. Some say Moses' mother Jochebed and his older sister Miriam were midwives, even though Miriam was just a little girl.

Right after Jesus was born, Luke tells us that that Mary "wrapped him snugly in strips of cloth" (Luke 2:7 NLT). The prophet Ezekiel also tells us about wrapping a baby like this (Ezek. 16:4). It must have made the baby feel good, like we do when we cuddle up in our blanket.

The prophet Ezekiel (16:4) also tells us that right after a baby was born, the midwife rubbed the baby with salt. A doctor in Roman times, named Soranus, said this was healthy. But in the Bible, salt was also connected to worshipping the Lord (Lev. 2:13). So perhaps salt reminded people to be thankful to God when a baby was born. Also, salt helps things last for a very, very long time. That is why an agreement with the Lord was called a "covenant of salt" (2 Chron. 13:5, NIV). And so rubbing a baby with salt could also mean wishing the baby a long life.

Church of Shepherds' Fields near Bethlehem, where the angels told the shepherds of Jesus' birth
(Shutterstock)

Babies in Jesus' day drank from clay bottles that looked like this one

Real milestones in the Holy Land. The Romans put these stone markers on the road to give people important information about where they were located; the "milestones" in our lives are the most important moments
(Courtesy of Miriam Feinberg Vamosh)

The Bible also tells us that people celebrated when a mother had a baby. When John the Baptist was born after his parents could not have children for many years, Luke (1:57, NLT) tells us "everyone rejoiced" with his mother Elizabeth.

In ancient Greece, the family of a newborn would hang symbolic items outside the house – olive branches for a boy and woolen threads for a girl. These were also a symbol. Perhaps the tree meant that the boy would work outdoors as a farmer, while mothers and grandmothers taught girls at home to weave wool into the clothing and blankets their family needed.

In the time of Jesus, among Jewish people, plants were also a symbol of the birth of a child. When a boy was born, the family would plant a cedar tree and when a girl was born, a pine tree. When the boy or the girl grew up and got married, they would use the branches of their trees to make the canopy under which the bride and groom would stand during the marriage ceremony.

A pine tree (Isa. 44:14); in Bible days, people planted pine trees to celebrate the birth of a daughter

What's in a Name?

Many stories in the Bible tell about naming a baby, because that was a way for parents to show that he or she belonged to their family (Isa. 43:1). When John was born, Elizabeth named him John because neighbors and relatives said, "the Lord had shown her great mercy" (Luke 1:58 NIV). What's the connection? In Hebrew, "John" is a whole sentence in a single word: Yohanan, which means "May the Lord be merciful." It's like a one-word prayer to God to watch over John.

There are many things about children's lives that are different today than in Bible times. But when a baby is born, all the people who love that baby still wonder: "What will this child turn out to be" (Luke 1:66 NLT), just like they did with John.

The name parents gave their new baby always said something important about the baby or how the mother felt about him or her. If we know what a name means in Hebrew, the Bible's original language, we can learn a lot about this idea. For example, Jacob's wife Leah said she felt "lucky" when one of her sons was born, and so she named him "Gad," which comes from a word meaning "lucky" in Hebrew. And here's a strange one: Job named one of his daughters Keren Happuch (Job 42:14), which means something like "makeup case"!

A cedar tree (Ps. 19:12); people planted cedars to celebrate the birth of a boy (Shutterstock)

Boy or Girl?

In ancient times, people often wanted to have baby boys rather than girls. That was because when a girl grew up and got married, she would go away to live with her husband's family. Sons, on the other hand, would stay close to their own parents and help the family make a living and so would their wives. When a son grew up, he was supposed to take care of his mother, especially if her husband had died. That was one of the reasons people were so happy when Jesus raised a widow's son from the dead because the son would be able to continue taking care of his mother. If a son had an

Salt (Ezek 16:4) (Shutterstock)

This mosaic made of small stones and pearls was given to the Basilica of the Annunciation in Nazareth by Christians in Japan. It shows Mary and Jesus (Courtesy of Eva Marie Everson)

important place in the community, it could make his mother feel very important, too. That's why we think the mother of Jesus' disciples James and John, the sons of Zebedee, asked Jesus: "In your Kingdom, please let my two sons sit in places of honor next to you, one on your right and the other on your left" (Matt. 20:20 NLT).

To sum up, let's remember that Scripture teaches that God knows who we are even before we are born: "You made all the delicate, inner parts of my body and knit me together in my mother's womb" (Ps. 139:13 NLT). The ancient sages also taught people that God is a part of making a baby: "There are three partners in the creation of man: the Almighty, his father and his mother."

When Does a 'Baby' Become a 'Boy'?

It takes a few years for a baby to grow up into a little boy or girl, to start walking and talking, eating grown-up food and knowing how to behave. One Bible word for very young children is *taf*, which comes from a Hebrew word describing how children move when they first start walking. In English, we have the same kind of word: "toddlers." To toddle means to walk unsteadily. Deuteronomy 1:39 (NIV) tells us that *taf*, or toddlers, "do not know good from bad."

When Paul the Apostle wanted to describe what a person was like before they became a believer, he compared that person to a little baby who "lives on milk [and] knows nothing about right teaching. But solid food is for those who are grown up. They are mature enough to know the difference between good and evil" (Heb. 5:13 NCV). We actually learn two things from Paul's words. Both of them were true in Bible days and still hold true: You only start eating solid food when you get older, and as you get older, you start learning the right thing to do.

Eating like the Adults

When Paul mentions children starting to eat "solid food," he was talking about an important milestone in their lives. That meant they no longer nursed milk from their mother's breast. Mothers usually nursed their babies for a long time because there were not a lot of other foods children could eat in those days. When babies stop nursing, it is called "weaning." People were very happy when their child was weaned, because it meant he or she was healthy, at a time when many children got sick easily and even died at a young age because they didn't have the medicines we do today to make them better. So they held a big party and invited everyone they knew. Abraham celebrated with a party like this when his son Isaac was weaned (Gen. 21:8).

King David himself wrote about the pleasant time of life after weaning: "I have calmed and quieted myself, like a weaned child who no longer cries for its mother's milk. Yes, like a weaned child is my soul within me" (Ps. 131:2 NLT).

Hannah celebrated on the day when she weaned her son Samuel (1 Sam. 1:24), because – like John's mother Elizabeth, as well as Sarah, Rachel and Samson's mother – Hannah had thought she could never have children. And here she was with a wonderful young son. When Samuel was three or four years old, she brought him to serve the Lord in a place called Shiloh, where the Israelites worshipped in those days. Even though Samuel was so young, the Bible says that he stopped living with his family and grew up in Shiloh, where he became a leader when he was very young and continued to lead until he was "old and gray" (1 Sam. 12:2).

Shiloh, where Samuel grew up and served in the Tabernacle
(Courtesy of Ancient Shiloh)

Don't Touch!

You've probably heard those words before. Not to touch something that's hot is one of the first things we learn when we are very small. That was true in ancient times as well, at least according to a legend about Moses. The Bible tells us that at first, Moses did not want to be a leader because he was not a good speaker (Ex. 4:10).

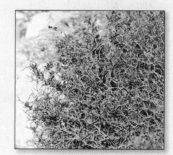

A thornbush (Ex. 22:6)

The wise men of old wondered whether something had happened to Moses that made it difficult for him to speak. This is what they imagined happened: One day, while Moses was still a toddler being raised by the Egyptian princess, he was sitting on Pharaoh's knee. Playfully, the small boy took Pharaoh's crown and put in on his own head. Pharaoh's magicians thought this meant Moses wanted to steal the crown from Pharaoh. To find out if this was true, they put in front of him one brazier (a small, portable fireplace) full of gold and one brazier full of hot coals. The magicians decided that if Moses took the gold, they would kill him, because that would have meant Moses wanted to steal Pharaoh's kingdom. But then, the Angel Gabriel came and moved the boy's hand to the hot coal and put it into Moses' mouth! By doing this, the Angel Gabriel saved Moses' life, but that also left him with speech problems.

Pharaoh's servants were very mean to test Moses in a way that could harm him. Just like today, parents and other people who want to keep children safe probably taught them when they were very small to stay away from things that are dangerous. That's why it was so special to think about a time, which the prophet Isaiah talked about, when we won't have to be afraid that a snake or a wild animal will hurt children. "In that day the wolf and the lamb will live together; the leopard will lie down with the baby goat. The calf and the yearling will be safe with the lion, and a little child will lead them all" (Isa. 11:6 NLT) and "the baby will play safely near the hole of a cobra. Yes, a little child will put its hand in a nest of deadly snakes without harm" (Isa. 11:8 NLT). This is hard to imagine, but that's why we remember this idea so well.

A myrtle bush (Isa. 41:29), the sweet-smelling and beautiful plant mentioned in our story
(Shutterstock)

The Teenage Years

When you become a teenager at age 13, you will probably be able to do many new things. But you will not be considered grown up yet. In Bible days, when a boy or a girl was between the ages of 11 and 13, they were considered as adults in most ways. Among the ancient Greeks, any time from 14 to 19, a boy was considered grown up when he began to wear the clothing men wore, called a toga. For a girl, that was the age she could be married. But getting older was also about how you should act. Starting at age 13, the ancient wise men said, a child could hear a voice inside him that told him to do the right thing.

The Elah Valley
(Courtesy of Eva Marie Everson)

Some biblical stories and legends tell us about the special deeds of important people in the Bible when they were young. These were things that we don't expect children to do (like a child playing with a snake or lying down next to a lion without being afraid), which makes the Bible's lessons even stronger. The Bible tells us that long before David was king, he was a shepherd boy who was brave and strong enough to fight and kill both a lion and a bear that attacked him or his flock (1 Sam. 17:34). And of course, David was very smart to use a sling-shot and a stone to kill the giant Goliath (1 Sam. 17:49-50).

A legend about Miriam, Moses' sister, says that she was only 5 years old when she came with her mother Jochebed to help the Israelite women have their children. One day, Pharaoh called Jochebed and Miriam to his palace to tell them they would have to kill all the baby boys that came into the world. The legend says Miriam stepped right up to Pharaoh, the most powerful man in Egypt, and said: "Because of your evil commandment, God will punish you!" By telling us this surprising story about the very young girl, the legend helps us understand how she would be a leader when she grew up (Mic. 6:4).

Sometimes young people had such great wisdom they could do things that even grown-ups could not, the way God gave young Daniel wisdom (Dan. 1:17). Jesus reminds us of this when he quotes Ps. 8:2: "You have taught children and infants to tell of your strength" (Matt. 21:16).

Herding sheep was one of the hard jobs children did in Bible times. The shepherd became an important Christian symbol, with the Bible saying that God is like a shepherd, (Ezek. 1:1-11 and Ps. 23:1). And Jesus said: "I am the good shepherd" (John 10:11). This ancient statue of a shepherd boy carrying a lamb across his shoulders was found in Caesarea
(Todd Bolen/BiblePlaces.com)

When Jesus was 12 years old, his parents took him to Jerusalem to celebrate Passover. When they were on their way home, they did not notice that Jesus was not with them. That's because in those days if you were on a journey, you would be just as happy walking along with your aunts and uncles as with your parents. But Mary and Joseph couldn't find Jesus among their relatives and friends, and they did start to worry. They finally found Jesus in the Temple, "sitting among the religious teachers, listening to them and asking questions" (Luke 2:46 NCV). Children went to school and asked their teachers questions, but it was an amazing sight to see Jesus sitting among a group of grown-ups and commenting on the Bible.

The ages of 11, 12 and 13 contained several "milestones" in Jesus' day. A father had to support his sons until they were 13 years old; after that, a boy

An Israeli boy with a biblical slingshot in the Elah Valley where David, not much older than this boy, killed the giant enemy of his people, Goliath, using a slingshot like the one shown here (1 Sam. 17:1-50)

was supposed to be able to earn his own living. When a boy was 12 years old, his father would take him to the Temple in Jerusalem, like Joshua in our little story wanted to do, for the older men to bless him in the Temple and pray he would learn the Bible and do good deeds.

Starting from one day after her 12th birthday, a girl who made a vow – a promise to do something, especially a promise to God – had to keep that vow just like an adult. Boys had to keep their vows, starting one day after their 13th birthday.

Today, Jewish people celebrate a special day for boys called a Bar Mitzvah, which means "son of the commandment" and for girls, a Bat Mitzvah, which means "daughter of the commandment." This day, when the 13-year-old boy or girl reads out of the Bible for the first time in front of the congregation, is so important that people imagine the tradition goes all the way back to the time of Jesus. But although the age of 13 was special for all boys in Jesus' day, as we have seen, it was not marked with the kind of ceremonies that Jewish people have nowadays.

The church in Cana, marking the site where Jesus turned water into wine at a wedding (John 2). Like today, weddings were one of the happiest milestones in people's lives
(Shutterstock)

Getting Married

If you lived in Bible times, when you were about 18 years old, it would be time for you to get married. Usually, your parents picked your bride or groom for you, although sometimes, if you saw someone you liked, you could convince your parents to let you marry that person, like Samson did (Judges 14:1-4). The boy, or the boy's parents, had to ask the girl's father for permission to marry her.

Sometimes the girl did not see her groom until right before they got married. That was what happened in the story of Rebecca in the Bible. Abraham, who lived in the land of Canaan, sent his servant Eliezer to a faraway land called Mesopotamia to find a wife for his son Isaac (Gen. 24:2-4). Eliezer found Rebecca, who was related to Abraham, and thought she would be perfect for Isaac. Rebecca agreed to come back with Eliezer to Canaan. Since it was a very long way, she rode a camel. When she first saw Isaac, she was still on the camel and she was so surprised (although we don't know exactly why) that she fell off the camel (Gen. 24:64) – or at least, that's what it says in Hebrew, the original language of the Bible.

This picture is in the church in Nain in Galilee, where Jesus went to a funeral and brought the young man who had died back to life
(Courtesy of Eva Marie Everson)

You can picture yourself going to the party in the story Jesus tells about a wedding (Matt. 25:1-12), because everyone in the village went to the wedding. The wedding celebration would take place at night. After the party, which included a big feast, everyone would walk alongside the bride to her new husband's home. Girls would hold torches or lamps (Matt. 25:1) to light the way, just as they had lit the way for the bridegroom to come to the feast. Someone would walk in front of them holding a chicken and a rooster, because eggs were a symbol of the many children they hoped the couple would now have.

The Garden Tomb in Jerusalem. Christians come to pray here and remember that Jesus was buried in a tomb that looked a lot like this one (John 19:41). In Roman times, people who went home to the Lord were often buried in caves. Lazarus, whom Jesus raised from the dead, was also buried in a cave (John 11:38)
(Shutterstock)

The Bible does not talk much about people celebrating their birthdays. Still, because of references to how old people were, or what they could do after a certain age – such as serve in the Tabernacle the way Samuel did, or in the Temple (2 Chron. 31:16) – we know birthdays were marked in some way.

Archaeologists digging in a place called Vindolanda in ancient Britain found a tablet inscribed with an invitation from a Roman officer's wife to another officer's wife to come to her house on her birthday. People wrote poems in honor of someone's birthday and then gave them the poem as a gift. The Bible tells us Pharaoh had a special feast for his birthday (Gen. 40:20), and we read that King Herod the Tetrarch celebrated his birthday (Matt. 14:6).

The only children's party mentioned in the Bible is to celebrate when they were weaned. The Bible doesn't talk about children having birthday parties. Maybe that's because most people did not consider children to be very important until they grew up.

Activities

Make a Biblical "Stone" Manger out of Paper Maché

A stone manger from Yad Hashmona

A manger is actually a feeding bin for animals. Many people imagine that the manger in which the baby Jesus was laid (Luke 2:16) was made out of wood. But in the Holy Land, people made mangers out of stone, because they didn't have much wood. Here's how you can make a manger that will look like stone to use your in nativity scene. On the next page, you'll see a picture of a model manger, along with instructions for making it. The model manger in the picture is about 11 inches long, 7 inches wide and 6 inches high.

- Select a rectangular cardboard box about the size you want your finished manger to be.
- Tear sheets of newspaper into strips about 2 inches wide.
- Prepare the flour-and-water mix. Since it will take several days to apply the strips, don't make more mix than you need for each application. For this manger, we used 1 cup of flour and 1 cup of water for each session. We also added 1/2 tablespoon of salt to the mixture. As you learned in this chapter, salt helps things last a long time.
- In your first few sessions, you can stuff small wads of the paper dipped into the paper maché mix into the corners so the inside won't be too square. Let dry well.
- Once you're done stuffing (that should take about two sessions), start covering the box, inside and out, with the strips dipped in the mix. You won't need to do the bottom, because you'll have straw inside that will cover it. Do about two layers at a time. You can bunch up the paper a little; you want the final result to look like rough-cut stone. You'll need about eight sessions (our manger took about two weeks to make) – usually you'll have to wait at least 24 hours between sessions to let the paper dry thoroughly.
- Next, it's time to paint. Use acrylic paint the color of Holy Land limestone, which is pale beige. We used three layers of paint, waiting a day or two between each application so the paint would dry completely. For your manger to last as long as possible, apply a layer of clear acrylic varnish.
- Finally, put your "straw" (from a craft store) in the manger and you're ready to place it in your nativity scene!

Chapter 7

Food

What Do We Care about Most?

Once upon a time, about 2,000 years ago, there were two boys named Judah and Simon who lived in a village in the Holy Land called Bethsaida. Like most of the villages around them, no one knew exactly how their village got its name. But people used to say it meant "house of fish" – perhaps because Bethsaida was very close to the Sea of Galilee, which was rich in fish.

Judah's father owned many fishing boats and had a big house. Judah and his family lived on the top level. From up there, Judah could see the Sea of Galilee sparkling in the distance. The servants lived in small rooms on the lower level, which opened onto a big courtyard. There was also a storeroom for the grain, wine and oil that the family's servants would buy in their local market and bring home on their donkey, which had its stable in the courtyard, too.

Simon's family did not live in the rich part of town. They lived down near the boat dock, in one room with a little courtyard in front. Some stairs outside the room led up to the roof. Simon would climb up to the roof before he went to sleep, so he could see his father setting off to fish, as he did every night when the lake was calm. Simon's father did not own even one boat; he worked on one of the boats that belonged to Judah's father. Simon was never hungry because there was always fish and bread to eat, which his mother made fresh every morning. Usually, Simon's mother had some fruit – carobs, dates or figs – drying on the mud-and-straw roof of their little house.

Simon's father was a good man. In the synagogue on the Sabbath, he would listen closely to the wise men – whether it was their village rabbi or teacher, or a wandering teacher – who got up to speak about God's word each week. He tried to obey God's laws and worked very hard. Judah's father liked Simon's father, and so he paid the village teacher to teach Simon right alongside Judah and the other boys who went to school at the synagogue every day.

Simon and Judah walked to school together every day. Like all the boys, they brought some food with them, which they would eat in a shaded corner of the synagogue courtyard. But Simon and Judah did not bring the same food to school. Judah,

being the son of a rich family, would bring a small piece of meat and hard-boiled eggs every day in a little cloth bag. Simon brought only two dried carobs. Now, carobs are sweet and very good for you and help keep you strong and active. But it's not the same as having meat and eggs, and Simon couldn't help wishing he could have the same thing, just for one day.

One morning, when the boat docked and Simon was helping his father pick up a net full of fish to take ashore, his face was very sad. "What's wrong, Simon?" his father asked. Simon told him he was tired of eating just two carobs every day when Judah had meat and eggs.

Simon's father did not answer right away. At first he was a little angry that Simon did not seem to be happy with what he had; after all, he never went hungry. But then Simon's father said: "Let me think about this until tomorrow, my son."

The next day, Simon went off to school as usual. He did not know that before his father went home to rest after his night of fishing, he went up the village path to see Judah's father at his big house. When Simon's father left, he was carrying a cooking pot Judah's wife had told the servant girl to give him. In the pot was about one pound of meat. In addition to his fishing business, Judah's father owned a small herd of sheep and could afford to eat meat at least once a week. Judah's father knew that

Simon's father was his best fisherman, so he did not mind giving him the pot of meat when asked.

When Simon's father got home, he told his wife about what he was going to do and asked her to put the pot in the oven, where the fire was dying down from the day's baking, to keep it warm.

When Simon came home from school, his father met him at the door of their little courtyard. "I have a surprise for you, my son," he said. He went to the oven and took out the pot. Simon followed him, curious. Simon's father placed it on the small wooden table in their one-room house. He turned to his son and said: "Take the lid off the pot." Simon did so and was really happy to see meat inside. With the pot lid in his hand, he turned to his father to give him a hug and thank him. His father hugged him back.

Just as Simon's mother was about to put the meat on a plate for Simon to enjoy, the hungry dog that hung around their house jumped up and stuck his head right inside the pot to grab the meat! Simon, his father and his mother all began chasing the dog, which was running around the courtyard, bumping into the walls, the doors and the oven and yelping because it could not get the pot off its head. Finally, the dog ran out of the courtyard and into the lane. "You wanted that meat so badly, my son! Let's not let the dog have it – run faster!" When people saw what was happening, they joined Simon's family and soon everyone was running after the dog with the pot on its head.

In a few minutes, it seemed to Simon that hundreds of people had joined the chase. The dog reached a little rise behind the village, with all the people behind it. But suddenly, the dog stopped running and began to shake and whimper. It was only a moment before everyone chasing him knew why. The earth itself had begun to tremble and shake! People who lived in Bethsaida – in fact, people who lived anywhere in the valleys around the Sea of Galilee – knew what that meant. It was an earthquake.

People turned around to look down at their village. All of the houses – the big ones belonging to rich people like Judah's father, and the small ones belonging to the simple fishermen like Simon's father – were swaying back and forth, and the next minute, the entire town fell down.

No one spoke for a long while. Even the dog (still with the pot on its head) was quiet. Everyone was wondering where they would sleep that night and where they would live, with their houses a pile of dust and rocks.

Finally, Simon's father spoke. Holding his son's hand, he said: "I am only a simple man. But I know something special happened today. We could have all been killed in our homes. But this silly dog, who took the meat we thought was so important, saved all of our lives! I think we should worry at least as much about keeping God's laws as my son and I worried about that meat. For I have heard it said from God's word: "If you pay attention to these laws and obey them carefully, the Lord your God will keep His agreement and show His love to you."*

*Deuteronomy 7:12 (NCV).
This story is based on a tale from Deuteronomy Rabbah, Lieberman edition, Jerusalem 1974, page 78 (Hebrew).

The Sea of Galilee, with the Valley of Bethsaida, at the far left, where the story in this chapter takes place.
(Courtesy of Eitan Rechtman)

Plenty to Eat in Bible Times

The two spies Joshua sent into the Holy Land brought back a gigantic bunch of grapes (Numbers 13:21–25). The above picture of two men carrying grapes became the symbol of Israel's Ministry of Tourism because according to the Bible, they were the first people to tour the land (Courtesy of Israel Tourism Ministry)

"...you and your families will eat, and you will enjoy all the good things for which you have worked, because the Lord your God has blessed you" (Deut. 12:7 NCV)

In this chapter you'll learn about some of the foods people ate in Bible days in the Holy Land. Of course, all people need food to stay alive and healthy. And time together at the table is a time to relax and enjoy God's blessings. But food and meals in the Bible are also mentioned often to show how God cares for us. For example, the verse in Ps. 23:5 (NCV) tells us: "You prepare a meal for me in front of my enemies," which is a way of saying with God's help, we don't have to worry when things go against us. Eating a meal together was a biblical way of sealing a very important agreement between people (Gen. 31:54). Also, since food was so important, when the Bible says someone "ate at your table" or "sat at your table," that meant you were supporting him or her (2 Sam. 19:28; 1 Kings 2:7; 2 Kings 25:29; Neh. 5:17).

Table of the Shewbread shown in the model of the Tent of Meeting in Timna Park in southern Israel (Todd Bolen/BiblePlaces.com)

What Did People Eat in Bible Days?

Grain, wine and oil were among the most basic foods God promised people they would have if they kept His commandments. Let's look more closely at each of these foods.

Grain

In Bible times, people grew mainly wheat and barley, which was ground to make flour and then baked into bread. Bread was the most basic food in those days. It was so important that the word "bread" came to mean all food.

A wheat field (Mark 2:23) in the Jezreel Valley in Galilee

In the Tabernacle in the desert, and later in the Temple in Jerusalem, there was a golden table with 12 very big loaves of bread on it (Lev. 24:5) that stood for the 12 Tribes of Israel, called the Table of the Shewbread. The loaves remind us of God's promise to provide bread for the people who worship Him faithfully (Isa. 33:16).

Bread can be baked quickly using just flour and water (you can try this yourself using the recipe in the Activities section of this chapter). That was the way the Israelites made it when they were in a hurry to escape from slavery in Egypt (Ex. 12:39), and the way the woman of En Dor made it when she hosted King Saul (1 Sam. 28:24).

Bedouin woman baking bread as people did in Bible times

(Nola Rin / Shutterstock.com)

In ancient times, it was hard work to get flour – women had to grind whole grain between two hard stones until it was soft and powdery. By the time of Jesus, they had

A Jewish coin from the second century AD, perhaps showing the Table of the Shewbread in the Temple, which held special bread baked by the priests (Lev. 24:5). (Courtesy of Classical Numismatic Group, www. cngcoins.com)

Grapes (Deut. 8:8; Isa. 5:6; John 15:2)

This heavy stone was used to crush olives to make olive oil. It is in Capernaum, a town where Jesus performed miracles

A donkey pushing a stone mill, crushing olives to produce oil. (Courtesy of the Eretz Israel Museum, Tel Aviv, Avitsur Collection)

begun to use a bigger grinder pushed around by a donkey. They did this every day, grinding just enough to last for that day. This was because the bread began to taste stale after only a few hours, since it didn't have anything in it to keep it fresh, as our bread today usually does.

You could also eat grain right off the stalk in early spring while it was still growing. Then it tastes almost like candy because it has a lot of sugar in it. That was probably how it tasted to Jesus and the disciples when they were plucking grain in the fields as they walked along one Sabbath day (Matt. 12:1). People also toasted grain in a frying pan over an open fire. This is what Ruth and Boaz had for lunch when they first met (Ruth 2:14).

Bread was also a very basic thing for children to eat. Jesus said "if your child asks for bread, would you give him a stone?" (Matt. 7:9). That reminds us that one of the ways to tell whether children were old enough to participate in certain preparations for the holiday of Passover was when they knew the difference between a stone and an egg. The test was simple: If children were given an egg and ate it, and given a stone and threw it away, then they were ready to join in.

Wine

Wine is mentioned in the Bible many times. Like bread, if people had all they needed, it meant that God was blessing them. When Moses sent the spies into the Promised Land to report to the Israelites about the country, they brought back a bunch of grapes that was so huge it took two men to carry it (Num. 13:23).

On the Jewish Sabbath table, both wine and bread are symbols of God's creation and goodness. In the Last Supper, the meal Jesus shared with his disciples before his crucifixion, Jesus also used the wine and the bread as symbols, and they are used in the same way to this very day in the communion service. After Jesus fed a crowd of people in Galilee with five loaves of bread and two fishes, Jesus said he was the bread of life (John 6:35), using bread as a symbol.

Oil

In Bible times, cooking oil came mainly from olives, which grow on beautiful trees with silvery-green leaves that live for hundreds of years. Like grain and wine, olive oil was one of the things people brought to the Tabernacle or the Temple to thank God for good things or to say they were sorry (a sacrifice). In the chapter on Health, you'll learn that olive oil was also used as a medicine by rubbing it on the skin, which was called anointing. Oil mixed with hot water was also given to children to drink to make them grow stronger.

The Seven Species

The Seven Species are seven plants that grow in the Holy Land (Deut 8:8): wheat, barley, grapes, figs, pomegranates, olives and honey. That last one might sound a bit strange, since the honey we know is not a fruit or grain like everything else on the list. Some people think the Bible was talking about honey made from dates – which is syrupy like bees' honey and also very sweet. In the Holy Land, in Bible times they didn't have sugar (which comes from a plant called sugar cane that did not grow in the Holy Land).

Pomegranates and figs grow in the Holy Land during the summer and ripen in the fall. Because they are harvested in the fall, people see them as one of the symbols of the "biblical Thanksgiving" – the Feast of Tabernacles, a harvest holiday that is celebrated in the autumn.

A pomegranate (Deut. 8:8)
(Shutterstock)

A date palm

Land of Milk and Honey

The Promised Land is described many times in the Bible by using two foods: milk and honey. Ezekiel said God told him: "I took a solemn oath that day that I would bring them out of Egypt to a land I had discovered and explored for them – a good land, a land flowing with milk and honey, the best of all lands anywhere" (Ezek. 20:6 NLT).

Sometimes we picture the Holy Land as one big desert – but this is not true. There is a big desert in the south, called the Negev, but even there, an ancient people called the Nabateans knew how to collect rainwater so they could grow grapes and fruit trees. The land around the Sea of Galilee is very fertile. One such area was Gennesaret (Mark 6:53). We know the fruit from this area was very sweet and rich in ancient times. Today, they grow bananas in the land of Gennesaret. The people of Bible times did not know about bananas, which came from Southeast Asia to Israel. Modern farmers in the Holy Land still grow crops people in Bible times knew about, like dates, and other things they did not know about – like oranges, lemons, sweet peppers and strawberries.

Ancient beekeepers making honey, after a picture in an Egyptian tomb

As we learned from the little story in this chapter, rich people and poor people did not eat the same things. Meat, for example, was eaten mostly on special occasions, and people usually kept the animals for their wool and their milk. Abraham served meat to the angels who came to him (Gen. 18:7). The woman of En Dor served meat to the king (1 Sam. 28:24). Jesus also told parables about a man who was so happy his lost son came home that he had a special meal that included lots of meat (Luke 15:27) and about another man who served meat at his son's wedding meal (Matt. 22:2-4). King Solomon's table had plenty of meat on it, according to 1 Kings 4:22-23. By the time of Jesus, many people kept chickens in their courtyards, although they were raised mainly for their eggs.

An Israeli beekeeper and his twin helpers
(Courtesy of Silk and Honey, Dovrat Hatavor)

Piles of salt on the Dead Sea shore
(Shutterstock)

Salt and Other Seasonings

Salt was the most important thing to add to food, both for flavor and because it kept the food fresh longer. Because it helps food last, it became a symbol of the way faith in God should last – a "covenant of salt," as we learned in the chapter on Milestones, meant an agreement that would last forever. Salt came from the Dead Sea, which is extremely salty. People served their salt in a little dish, not in shakers like we use. Sometimes it had a little dirt in it, which would get thrown out after the meal. That's what Jesus meant when he called people "salt of the earth" (Matt. 5:13) and talked about salt losing its saltiness (when only the dirt was left).

Other Important Foods in the Bible

Eggs were said to be the second best food for people after meat. Eggs in a kind of porridge was one of the foods given to very young children after they had stopped nursing, usually when they were two or three years old.

Hyssop
(Shutterstock)

Lentils, which are related to peas, were probably the most common food after bread in Jesus' day. Lentils were on the list of foods David's men ate when they were fighting in the desert (2 Sam. 17:28), and Ezekiel baked them into bread (Ezek. 4:9).

The best known Bible story about lentils is the lentil stew that Jacob prepared (Gen. 25:29). His brother Esau was so hungry that he sold his birthright (the blessing and extra share of a father's possessions the oldest son received) to Jacob in exchange for some lentil stew.

Chickpeas, another food related to lentils, are very nourishing. The prophet Isaiah mentions them (Isa. 30:24), although they are called "mash" or "fodder" in English, because the people who translated the Bible probably didn't have chickpeas in their country and didn't know exactly what it was. Chickpeas are still one of the most basic foods in Israel and the other Bible lands. When you are in Israel, you can try falafel and hummus, two delicious foods that are both made of chickpeas.

An olive tree in Galilee

There were many different kinds of vegetables in Bible days, not all like those we eat today. The Bible says that when the Israelites were wandering in the desert and didn't have much to eat, they wished they had cucumbers like they used to eat in Egypt (even though they were slaves then) (Num. 11:5). But that "cucumber" was not like the vegetable by that name that we know today (see page 80). They had onions and garlic, but no tomatoes or green or red peppers. They also didn't have potatoes, or corn on the cob, which came from the other side of the world in those days, from North and South America, which people in the ancient Holy Land probably didn't even know existed.

People also ate plenty of fish. Perhaps the most famous story in the Gospels about eating fish is when Jesus multiplied two fish and five loaves of bread, and fed 5,000 people (Matt. 14:17-21). Fish were also caught in rivers and in the Mediterranean Sea, and were raised in special pools built in ancient times that archaeologists have found near the seashore in some places, such as the ancient port of Caesarea, and even in the Judean mountains.

Clay model of a boat, about 3,000 years old, found at Achziv on the shore of northern Israel (IAA)

Jesus also ate a piece of broiled fish in Jerusalem after the resurrection in the presence of his disciples (Luke 24:42). Archaeologists have turned up an amazing find in Jerusalem's City of David from many centuries before Jesus' time – more than 10,000 fish bones!

Mealtimes

People usually ate two meals a day in the time of Jesus – morning and evening. Some people thought having a piece of bread first thing in the morning (which meant soon after sunrise, when farming families would get up) would keep them healthy, and help them work and learn and teach Bible better. Others said it was best for adults to wait until "the fourth hour" (that meant 10-11 o'clock) to eat the first meal of the day. The second meal was in the late afternoon, when people came home from work, while it was still light. Even though it was early, this was the last meal of the day, since everyone went to bed very soon after sunset.

A special drinking cup shaped like a bull, about 3,000 years old (IAA)

Children didn't always sit with their parents at the table, and moms seem to have been too busy serving to sit down (Luke 4:39; Luke 10:40). But at special meals, like the one in the verse at the top of this chapter, or Sabbath and holiday meals, the whole family ate together. These days, we like to picture children sitting at the table with their parents as a happy time, the way Ps. 128:3 describes the family: like an olive tree with little trees coming out around the bottom of the main trunk.

The Sabbath meal was different than the regular evening meal in many ways. One way of making it more special was to eat after dark. That led to the lighting of lamps at the meal, and eventually to a special blessing over the lamps to mark the beginning of the Sabbath. Today, Jewish women still say a blessing over Sabbath candles.

The mosaic of the Loaves and Fishes in the church that marks the site where Jesus fed 5,000 people with two fish and five loaves of bread (Matt. 14:13-21)

The Passover meal was also a special time for children – not only did they eat delicious food, but during the meal they learned all about how God brought the Israelites out of Egypt from slavery to freedom. Because a story called the Hagaddah was (and still is) told during the meal, it takes a long time. As we learned in the chapter on Toys and Games, children would be allowed to play games at the table (for example, with nuts) to keep them awake and interested for the whole meal.

People usually ate in the main room of their home. But if they had invited a big group of people and the weather was nice, sometimes they would eat outside in their courtyard, where there was more space. One ancient parable that talks about guests at a festive

Entrance to a food storage cave at Shiloh in the Holy Land. Caves kept food cool and fresh (Courtesy of Ancient Shiloh)

Carobs, a very healthy fruit

A quail, the kind of bird God sent the Children of Israel in the wilderness so they would have food to eat (Ex.16:13)
(Shutterstock)

This street from Jesus' time is in Bethsaida, where people once met Jesus and where the little story in this chapter takes place. Scholars say Bethsaida means "house of fish"
(Courtesy of Miriam Feinberg Vamosh)

dinner teaches us that they had "potluck dinners" (where everyone brings something from home to share) in the time of Jesus. Ten people were invited to a meal and each of them brought a different food. One guest brought a big fish, the second brought little fish, the third brought salty fish, the fourth brought boiled cabbage, the fifth brought beets, the sixth brought eggs, the seventh brought cheese, the eighth brought ox meat, the ninth brought deer meat and the tenth brought a chicken or pheasant. The teachers of this parable were actually trying to say that studying the word of God is like a rich meal, and each person brings something special to it.

Jesus reminds us that it's also important to invite people who don't have enough to eat to come to your meal, not just your friends and neighbors (Luke 14:12-15).

Can you picture almost lying down while you eat? That's the way people often ate in ancient times, especially at festive meals, or if they were wealthy and had servants to bring them their food. They didn't lie down like you do in bed, though. They reclined – leaning on one elbow. Jesus ate this way at the home of Simon the Leper in Bethany (Mark 14:3) and at the Last Supper (Matt. 26:20). People reclined on special couches alongside their tables. The table had three sides, shaped like a U, so the servants could reach everyone at the table.

One rule of politeness was to allow the most important person at the meal to take his place first, and then the next most important, and so on. Once, in Jerusalem, when Jesus was having a meal with an important man, he noticed how people were trying to pick the most important place at the table for themselves (near the host). He used their behavior to teach a lesson: He told a story about a wedding dinner where many people had decided that they themselves deserved the place of honor, but then the host came and made them get up if someone more important came in (Luke 14:7-10). Jesus wanted to use this story to teach people to be humble.

Washing your hands was also a custom before a meal (Mark 7:4; Luke 11:38). If the diners were wealthy, a servant would walk around with a bowl, beginning with the most important person at the meal. At the Last Supper, the washing of feet is mentioned. People used to have to wash their feet quite often when they came home, because they wore sandals and the roads in the Holy Land are dusty. That was usually a servant's job. Jesus took the job of washing everyone's feet at the Last Supper (John 13:6-11). Since he was their leader, this was the opposite of what people expected, so his act could also teach them an important lesson about humility.

Fruits and vegetables grown today in the desert in the south of Israel
(Isa. 35:1-2)
(Courtesy of Aaron Vamosh)

Blessings

The Gospels tell us Jesus said a blessing before a meal many times: before he multiplied the loaves and fishes, for example, in Matt. 14:19, in Emmaus (Luke 24:30) and at the Last Supper (Matt. 26:26). The blessing Jesus said is probably the same one said today by Jewish people before a meal: "Blessed are You O Lord our God, King of the Universe, who brings forth bread from the earth." If more than three people were eating together, everyone was invited to say the blessing, remembering that Ps. 34:3 (NCV) says: "Glorify the Lord with me, and let us praise his name together."

When the meal was over, people said (and still say) blessings called "Grace after Meals." This is a long song, which asks God to bless the host, thanks God again for the food, for His teachings and care for us, and special prayers for Jerusalem. Some of these prayers come in the form of Psalms. After the Last Supper, Jesus and the disciples "sang a hymn" (Matt. 26:30; Mark 14:26) – that was probably the Grace after Meals.

The Bible sets down many rules about food, especially about the animals, birds and fish that people should and shouldn't eat. These were divided into two main groups – clean and unclean. There was also a rule against boiling the meat of a young animal in the milk of its mother (Ex. 23:19; 34:26; Deut. 14:21), perhaps with the thought that the mother animal would be sad if she knew. In Peter's vision about clean and unclean animals when he was on the roof of Simon the Tanner (Acts 10:9-16), the animals stood for Peter's mission to bring faith in Jesus to gentiles.

Bread, fish and grain were important foods in Bible times (Shutterstock)

Some people think that the forbidden foods are not good for you. Other people say God forbade some foods because He wanted the Israelites to act differently than their neighbors so they would remain apart from them and better able to remember God's laws.

On the Market

Markets were where people bought almost everything they needed, and also changed their money there if they had come from another country. Big cities had huge markets – or at least, these lively places must have looked huge if you came from a small village. One man who wanted to describe the market in the Galilee town of Sepphoris was probably exaggerating just a little when he said he saw "180,000 markets for pudding dealers."

That really would have been a busy place! A busy market was a sign that the city and its people were doing well. The prophet Zephaniah warns that because people worshiped idols, the markets in Jerusalem would be destroyed (Zeph. 1:11).

Markets also had restaurants, where people could buy food or bring their own food for someone to cook for them. The big

Olive groves overlooking the Sea of Galilee

market was divided into different sections with names that came from the main thing sold in each section.

Some marketplaces also had temples to false gods, and it was very hard for people who believed in God to go to such markets. Sometimes people decided not to go to these places at all. But if they had to go, they were told to make sure no one would think by mistake they were worshipping idols. For example, you would be careful not to bend down to tie your sandal near the statue of a false god so no one would think you were bowing down to it.

Clowns also performed in markets, and it was said they deserved a special blessing because they could make people laugh when they were sad, and get angry people to stop arguing with each other.

And argue they did! If you wanted to buy something, you would ask the seller how much it cost and then you would probably offer to pay less. This discussion, called bargaining, went on until buyer and seller reached a price they agreed

A man selling fruit in the Jerusalem farmers market
(Courtesy of Dalia Bernstein)

on. People do the very same thing nowadays when they shop at the colorful markets in the Old City of Jerusalem, Acre or Lydda.

Lentils, a nourishing food that biblical people ate (Gen. 25:34; 2 Sam. 23:11-12)
(Shutterstock)

The Bible says it is a sin against God to cheat when you weigh things in the market or to give people less than the amount they were paying for (Lev. 19:35-36; Prov. 16:11). The prophet Micah (6:11) got angry about people cheating in the market.

If you lived in Bible times, you might have gone to the market with your parents, like the little girl, Martha, in our chapter on Toys and Games. Or you might have even worked in the market. As you learned in the chapter on Toys and Games, Jesus describes children "sitting in the market place calling to each other 'We played music for you, but you did not dance; we sang a sad song, but you did not cry'" (Matt. 11:16-17; Luke 7:31-33 NCV). Since Jesus used this picture as a symbol, people must have seen children really doing this. Do you think those children might have been talking to each other about the games they had played when they were allowed to take a break or before work?

Armenian cucumbers – these were the biblical cucumbers the Israelites missed eating after they left Egypt (Num. 11:5)

Activities

(Shutterstock)

Make Your Own Biblical Bread

Ingredients
4 cups flour
7 tablespoons vegetable oil
3/4 cup of water

1. Mix the oil into the flour. Add the water to the flour mix and stir well. Add a little more water if needed until you can stretch the dough a little without tearing it.
2. Knead the dough. Divide it into balls a little smaller than a tennis ball and then pat them down until they are flat and about half an inch thick.
3. Put them on a baking sheet and bake in a preheated oven at 350 F. Turn them over when they start to brown (about 3 minutes). They're ready when they've started to brown on the other side (about two minutes later) or, fry them in a frying pan at medium heat in a little olive oil for about two minutes on each side.

Make a Plate of Biblical Foods

You can put these foods on your dinner table and share with your family. But which of the following foods won't be on it?
You'll find stickers with these foods in the pocket in the back of this book. Find the stickers that show biblical foods and stick them on this plate.

Dates
Figs
Potato chips
Bread
Pizza
Bananas
Olives
Sugar
Tomatoes
Cheese
Eggs
Chocolate chip cookies
Lemons
Strawberries
"Cucumbers"

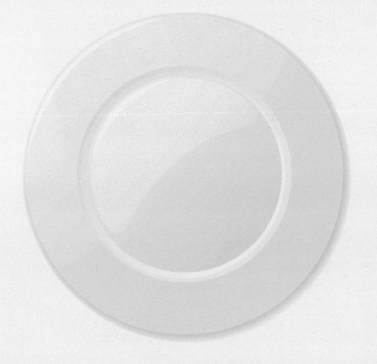

Chapter 8

Water

Abigail Finds a Spring

Abigail put up her hand to shade her eyes from the sun as it peered over the hills east of her home on the desert's edge. She skipped to the front of her flock, leaving her faithful dog, Gray, to nudge the last of the sheep and goats out of the stone corral. She would be first at the spring today, before her friends. After she watered the flock, there would be plenty of time for talk and play as the animals grazed peacefully nearby.

A soft breeze was coming from the south – a good sign that more rain was on the way to follow the first winter rain, called the *yoreh*, which had recently ended the long, dry summer.

For weeks before the yoreh, everyone had been looking heavenward, waiting impatiently for the first rain in eight months. Eight whole months without a drop of water from the sky. People were starting to worry because the springs were giving less and less water with each passing day. It was all anyone could talk about. "Will the animals have enough to drink? How will we wash and cook? And what will we drink?"

"The south wind brings showers and makes the pastures grow," Uncle Simeon offered at yesterday's evening meal. As they dipped their bread into their stew, the family nodded gravely at the truth of the old saying.

Abigail was pleased that she would be able tell everyone later that she had noticed the south wind blowing; it had already brought a light shading of green to the hills. She looked up and spotted a few clouds scuttling across the bright blue morning sky. They didn't look like the hollow kind that, according to her father, filled with water poured from heaven, but more like the kind the sun would burn off by midday. Still, she knew that at this time of year, the weather could change any minute.

Abigail was 10 years old, and she already knew almost everything she had to know about her most important work in the family. It was her job each day to take the sheep and goats to pasture beyond their little house at the edge of the village of Krayot, on the slopes of the Judean hills facing the vast wilderness of the Negev desert. She could count high enough to know that all 30 of her sheep were with her.

And just like King David, who was a shepherd when he was a young boy, she was an expert with a slingshot, which she used to keep away the wild foxes that preyed on her sheep.

During the rainless summer months, Mama told Papa she would not let Abigail venture out alone with the flock. Even now, after the first rain had come, the springs were far from overflowing, and Abigail had heard her Mama telling Papa he should send Abigail's big brother with her: "What will she do all by herself when she gets to our spring and finds the tent-dwellers have got there before her?"

The tent-dwellers, whose life in the desert had made them fierce, would often take the water from the village spring when their usual watering holes ran dry.

"She'll know what to do," Papa had replied. As he had taught Abigail and her sisters and brothers, God had provided many springs in the wilderness. When Hagar, Sarah's servant girl, had to wander in the desert with her son Ishmael not far from this very spot, God showed her a hidden spring.

Today, it looked as if Abigail was about to find out whether Papa was right. In the valley below, where only yesterday Abigail and the other village shepherdesses had drawn their water, were women from the desert-dwellers, with their menfolk at their side. Abigail looked back along the trail to see if any of her friends were following yet, but she was still alone. She had to think quickly before the people below saw her.

"Yes, yes, I've got it," she murmured as a big smile lit her face. She headed off the animals by shunting the lead sheep off the

main path down the valley and moved them toward a trail leading further into the wilderness, not down into the valley. Gray perked his ears up at the sudden change in plans, but he trusted his little mistress, and while Abigail led the sheep, Gray nipped at the heels of the last of the goats to keep them on the new path.

Abigail had remembered her Mama's worried advice this morning to head further along the slope before heading into the valley. Last year, her first year herding alone, her mother had gone with her to make sure she knew how to reach "the secret valley." It was a much longer trudge, and the sun was much higher in the sky by the time Abigail began leading the flock down there, where the spring was surrounded by high rock walls.

As the opening to the hidden valley came into full view, she realized that again, she was not alone. But this time, she smiled with relief. In the distance she saw a mama mountain goat, an ibex, with her babies. The mother goat was pawing patiently at the ground, and at her feet, a tiny pool of water was forming. Abigail knew that if the big ibex had found water right there at her feet, then upstream in the hidden valley, there would be enough water for her own flocks, far from the prying eyes of others.

The ibex raised their heads at the sound of the bleating sheep as Abigail led the flock past the little waterhole they had created. They scampered off up the slope, the mother nudging her little ones ahead of her on the path. "I hope they had enough to drink," Abigail thought to herself. As she led the way into the narrow passage, she could already hear the delicious sound of trickling water.

Abigail would have her own story to tell tonight at the evening meal. She knew her father and her uncles would immediately begin planning how to approach the desert-dwellers and warn them away from the spring that had belonged to Krayot since their first ancestors had settled there. She felt proud to be able to help the family and the village to protect their water.

"Then God opened Hagar's eyes, and she saw a well full of water. She immediately filled her water container and gave the boy a drink" (Gen. 21:19 NLT)

The opening of a water cistern cut into the rock at ancient Shiloh (Josh. 18:1)
(Courtesy of Ancient Shiloh)

The Sea of Galilee, the biggest lake in the Holy Land, as seen from the Mensa Christi Church, which marks a famous place where Jesus met the disciples after the Resurrection (John 21)

The water tunnel at Megiddo, which people dug about 2,700 years ago to reach the nearby spring
(Todd Bolen/BiblePlaces.com)

Ibex (wild goats) in the desert, like the animals in our story
(Courtesy of Uri Bernstein)

Zipporah, Rebecca and Rachel were among the girls and young women of the Bible who had to draw water from a well or a spring every day of their lives. Moses helped Zipporah and her sisters fight off a band of men who came to steal their water (Ex. 2:15-17), and Jacob lifted a heavy stone cover off Rachel's well so she could get water (Gen. 29:10). The Bible also tells us that Rebecca had just gotten some water from the well to pour into a trough (a feeding dish) for her animals – or perhaps to take home for washing and drinking – when Abraham's servant Eliezer, whom she had not met before, asked her for a drink (Gen. 24:15-20). Eliezer was no ordinary stranger; Abraham had sent him from a faraway land to find a wife for Abraham's son, Isaac. When Eliezer saw what a hard worker Rebecca was, and how kind she was to him, a stranger, watering his camels after their long journey, he decided she was the one he had prayed for God's help to find!

In Bible days, and today, too, if you don't have enough water, it can be very dangerous. That's why, in the story of Hagar in the desert with her small son Ishmael, she was so afraid that he would die of thirst that she started to cry. But then an angel of the Lord came to Hagar and showed her a hidden spring (Gen. 16:7). By giving her thirsty son a drink, she saved Ishmael's life.

These days, when you're thirsty, you don't have to work hard like the people did in Bible times. Most of us only have to turn on the faucet in the kitchen or bathroom, or even press a button on the refrigerator door – and out comes as much clean, drinkable water as we need!

People who live in the desert – like Hagar in the Bible or Rachel, the little shepherd girl in the story you just read – had to find springs of water in order to live. But how can there be a spring in the dry desert? This is how it works: The water in the ground starts out as rainfall (yes, rain does fall in a desert, but not very often). When it rains and the drops fall to the earth, part of the water turns into rivers, springs and ponds. But some of the water also sinks right into the ground, and you might not even know it is there. Some of this groundwater ends up in a sort of water trap, called the aquifer. A trap like this can only form where there is a certain kind of ground, such as clay, that stops the water from sinking down past the surface, and where the rock is a type called limestone. The trapped water then looks for a crack in the rocks and if it can find one, it flows out at that spot. That's how a spring is formed.

In Israel, rain usually falls only during certain months of the year – from October until around the end of April. Before the first rain arrives to end the dry season (Ps. 84:6), the ground is very hard and cracked. But after it rains, the soil gets softer and muddier, so the farmers can start plowing and sowing. The last rain is very important for the fruit trees and the wheat. But if it happens to come at the wrong time, the raindrops can knock the budding fruit right off the trees and wash the young grain off the stalks.

Because water was so important for survival, people sometimes quarreled with each other about it. The Bible tells us there were two places in the wilderness where the wandering Israelites quarreled bitterly with their leader, Moses, because they were afraid they were going to die of thirst. Moses hit some nearby rocks with his tall walking stick, and water came flowing out. But these places were called Meribah, which in Hebrew means "quarrel," so that no one would forget what happened there (Ex. 17:1-7).

In the desert, people sometimes fought to protect a well they had dug deep into the ground (all the way to the aquifer), because they didn't want anyone else to use it. That's what happened when Isaac's men dug a well in the desert and shepherds from another tribe came to say the water was theirs. Isaac had to move to another well, like Abigail did in our story (Gen. 26:19-22).

Thirsty for the Word

Rain was like a very special gift. In fact, the Book of Proverbs calls a person who talks about giving gifts but never actually gives them, "clouds and wind without rain" (Prov. 25:14 NIV).

According to an ancient story, a man was wondering about the fact that different religions celebrate different holidays. He wanted to know whether there were any holidays that everyone celebrated. So he asked a famous wise man: "You have festivals and we have festivals, but when you rejoice, we do not; and when we rejoice, you do not. When do we all rejoice?" The wise man, whose name was Rabbi Joshua, answered that there was one "holiday" when everyone rejoiced – when it rained! He taught the man some verses of Psalms, including Ps. 66:1, which says "everything on earth, shout with joy to God," (NCV) explaining that it meant that rain falling was a time of joy for everyone in the world.

Water was so important to life that, like bread, as you learned in the chapter on Food, the Bible used it as a symbol. One example of this is when Jesus met a woman one day at a well in an area called Samaria (see map on page 5) and asked her for a drink. The woman learned that the water from the well would save her life, but that she should also think about God like a well of water that would never go dry (John 4:7-13) If she did, she would understand that God could save her spiritual life the way real water saved her physical life.

The prophet Isaiah also wrote about water as a symbol of God's truth, when he said "all you who are thirsty; come and drink" (Isa. 55:1 NCV).

The aqueduct (a bridge that carried a water channel) leading to Caesarea (Acts 8:40)
(Shutterstock)

A stream in the desert at Ein Avdat in southern Israel (Ps. 78:16, Ps. 126:4)
(Shutterstock)

The Arugot Stream in the Judean Desert

A Bedouin woman pouring water for her flock, like Rebecca in the Bible (Gen. 24:15-20)
(Dan Peretz / Shutterstock.com)

At this ancient well outside of biblical Beersheba, people remember that Isaac found water here (Gen. 26:25)
(Todd Bolen/BiblePlaces.com)

In fact, people were taught that once, when the wandering Israelites quarreled with Moses because they had been searching for water for three days and could not find any (Ex. 15:22) – they were really upset because "water" was a symbol for hearing a Bible lesson! That is why the Jewish people started reading the Bible at least three times a week (on Saturdays, Mondays and Thursdays) – so they wouldn't get "thirsty for the word" by going more than three days without the Bible. And that's why the parents of many children read the Word with them.

A special kind of water wheel called an antilya , once common in Bible lands
(Photo: American Colony, courtesy Arie Fishman, Medva Surveying and Engineering)

Activities

A Picture to Color

Have fun coloring this picture. You can use a blue crayon or pencil to follow the water from the rain, to the underground layer it follows and then to the well that people dug so they could get to the water, like the man and the woman you see here.

Make an Aquifer Using Chalk, Flour and Small Stones

Where did the water come from that the little shepherdess in our story drew from the well, and the spring that saved Hagar's life in the Bible? How does a spring work? Make your own to show how rain sinks into the ground, and comes out where there's a layer of clay the water can't go through.

Materials

1 disposable plastic cup (you can paint or color the plastic cup in earth colors)
Small amount of flour
Very small stones
A pitcher or glass with "rain water"
A plate to catch your "spring water" from below

Now make your spring:

1. Make two very small holes in the side of the cup one above the other with a little space in between.

2. Place a single layer of your tiny stones in the bottom of the cup, covering the lower hole from the inside.

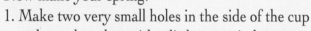

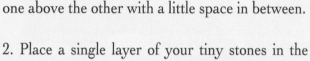

3. Place a layer of flour above the stones. Make sure the flour doesn't cover the upper hole.

4. Above the flour, fill the cup with small stones to the top. Now make it rain! Pour some water over the "ground" in your cup and watch it come out the upper hole – your spring. It won't come out the lower hole because flour holds it back.

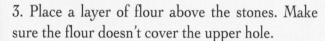

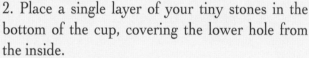

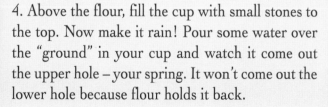

(Ccourtesy of Yonatan Dubinsky)

Chapter 9
Health

Grandma's Story

Grandma was crouched in front of the oven, knees bent, resting her broad bottom slightly on her ankles, pressing the dough patties of their daily bread onto the inside walls of their courtyard oven. As usual, the children were milling around her as close as she would let them come while she was baking in front of the hot oven. From time to time she would pinch off a bit of dough and give it to them to make into little shapes. But they wanted more. They wanted to hear The Story.

As she worked, her tunic had fallen aside ever so slightly to reveal the lower part of a long, white scar on her leg. The children knew how she got the scar – they had heard The Story a hundred times, at least! They knew grandma had quite a limp – she often sent one of them off to the sandal-maker to have him sew another patch of leather to the sandal on which she walked more heavily because of that childhood accident. But they never tired of hearing the tale. In fact, neither did the grown-ups, who asked her to tell it every time visitors came to her home town of Capernaum.

Just yesterday, the children had begged to hear it. "Tomorrow, children, tomorrow," Grandma had said. So she wasn't surprised when the little group of cousins put aside their dough-animals and chimed, almost in unison, "Grandma, tell us The Story! You promised."

"Fine, children. I'll finish the baking and we'll sit together – over there," she said, pointing to a shady spot far away from the oven. The children scampered over, and when she was done with her work, she rose, limped over to them, and crouched down again.

"Well, I wasn't much older than you," she began, her eyes resting fondly on the eldest granddaughter in the group, age 11. "And I was a wild one! Instead of helping my mother with the weaving and baking like my sisters, I was always off somewhere running around. And then one day, I got it into my head to see if I could climb that date palm tree – the one right there by the water," she said, pointing toward the Sea of Galilee shore just beyond the last houses of the village. "If the date harvesters

could do it, I thought, why couldn't I?"

"I had almost reached the top when all of a sudden..." Grandma stopped, as she always did at this point. "Ayeeeeeeeeeeeee," she cried out. The children's eyes grew wide, as if they could see her as one of them – a frightened little girl tumbling out of a tall tree. "Down and down and down, I went scraping and scratching every part of me. Oh, the pain! The pain!" Grandma's eyes filled with tears.

"Everyone thought I was dead. Even I thought I was dead! I thought any minute they were going to wrap me up in a cloth from head to toe and put me in a burial cave! But then, I thought, how could I be dead...because here I am thinking about being dead. Oh, I thought to myself, my mama will be so angry. I couldn't open my eyes, but I could hear her though. She was crying her heart out.

"I felt my papa pick me up gently. He carried me home. Someone had unrolled the bedding and they laid me on the bed," she continued.

"Of course, as you all know, your great-grandfather, Jairus, was a very important man; he was the leader of the synagogue. I was his only child, and so as soon as people heard what had happened, they came streaming to our house. I could hear them whispering.

"The midwife – who not only delivered all the babies in Capernaum, but also took care of anyone who was sick or injured – must have come, because the next thing I knew I could feel something burning my skin," Grandma said. The children wrinkled up their noses at this. They knew what she meant – Grandma always kept on hand a paste made of unripe dates to rub on all their scrapes and scratches.

"Oh, it burned, it burned… Ayeeeeeeee," Grandma let out another screech, and one of the smaller children giggled nervously until silenced by her older brother. "I thought I was crying out, but I wasn't. I couldn't. I don't know why. I also heard them arguing about what to put on my sores – one said beeswax and pitch, the black stuff from the Dead Sea. Another said honey.

"And I heard some say..." she let her voice fall to a whisper, "...'she's dead.' They even brought the wailing women and the flute-players, which meant that everyone in Capernaum must have known what happened."

"Of course, they did, grandmama. Great-grandpa Jairus had told everyone," one of the older boys cried out. Grandma glared at him, and so did all the other children. The best part was coming, and Grandma didn't like being interrupted. This was Grandma's favorite part of the story and the children knew it.

"Just then, my father, your great-grandpapa Jairus, came into the room. And he wasn't alone. I couldn't see that, of course, because don't forget I couldn't open my eyes, but I could hear everything. Suddenly, the noise stopped – no more wailing, no more saying Psalms, no more flute-playing.

"And then I felt someone touch my arm. It wasn't like the touch of the midwife with her ointments and her lambs-wool bandages, or even like my mother's touch. But just like the touch of my mother's hand, I can still feel that touch, to this day.

"I heard a man's voice, smooth and low, say to me 'get up, little lamb...' And I, who a moment before couldn't even open my eyes, opened them, just like that! And there was that man. He was smiling, standing next to him were some of his friends, and so were my father and mother. Mama was weeping, but this time, I knew it was because she was happy."

The children all sighed when they heard the part about the special man, whose name was Jesus. Everyone knew about him by then. From that day forward, Grandma said, people were always stopping her and the other people Jesus had healed, asking to hear all about their amazing experience.

And the story has never been forgotten, and is told all around the world to this very day.

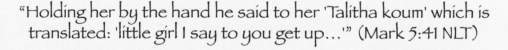

The Pools of Bethesda, where Jesus healed a man who could not walk (John 5:1–8)
(Todd Bolen/BiblePlaces.com)

Women carrying water jars as women did in Bible times
(Shutterstock)

"Holding her by the hand he said to her 'Talitha koum' which is translated: 'little girl I say to you get up...'" (Mark 5:41 NLT)

We all know people who get sick – that's just part of everyday life. It was that way in Bible days, too. And so stories about people who got sick, hurt or died are mentioned in the Bible only when something special happened, like healing miracles, as when God healed Miriam, Moses' sister (Num. 12:13) or Naaman the Syrian (2 Kings 5:1-14) and the many stories about sick people that Jesus healed. Sometimes the Bible tells us the story because the sickness or the healing happened to a famous person, like King Hezekiah or King Josiah.

Children, of course, also got sick. Sadly, children's lives were often short in Bible times, because people did not have the medicines or knowledge that we have today. In fact, most people did not live as long as they do nowadays. But sometimes children miraculously got better, such as the widow's son healed by the prophet Elijah (1 Kings 17:17-24) or the little girl Talitha (as you probably guessed, she was the model for the grandma in this chapter's story) and the royal official's son (John 4:46-50), both of whom Jesus healed.

Archaeology can help us learn what kind of medical problems people had in Bible times. For example, women had to carry heavy loads, like water pots or firewood, on top of their heads, and this caused them to get little growths on their neck bones that were often painful. The bones in their ankles also show how much time they spent crouching down, probably in front of a cooking fire or an oven. As in our other chapters, we can also learn about health and medicine from the wise men of the Talmud and other ancient sources.

This chapter will help you understand what people in Bible days thought about illness, what kinds of illnesses people, especially children, got, and what medicines they may have taken to get better. You'll see pictures of the places in the Holy Land where some of the Bible stories about sickness and healing took place. You'll also learn how important prayer is when you get sick.

Prayer

When you were sick in those days, even if you were taking medicine (which was mostly made from different kinds of plants), the Bible teaches that prayer was very important. That's because God said: "I will heal" (Deut. 32:39 NIV). Once, when God was very angry with Miriam and Aaron, Moses' sister and brother, Miriam got a skin disease the Bible calls leprosy. Moses said: "Please, God, heal her!" (Num. 12:13 NCV). James, the brother of Jesus and leader of the church in Jerusalem, taught: "Are any of you sick?

This 2,000-year-old child-sized shirt was found at Masada. Herbs believed to keep children healthy were sewn into special little pockets at the corners
(IAA)

You should call for the elders of the church to come and pray over you, anointing you with oil in the name of the Lord. Such a prayer offered in faith will heal the sick, and the Lord will make you well" (James 5:14-15 NLT).

You can find some of the best prayers for health in the Book of Psalms. For example, "Lord, have mercy on me because I am weak. Heal me, Lord, because my bones ache. I am very upset. Lord, how long will it be? Lord, return and save me; save me because of your kindness" (Ps. 6:2-4 NCV). When you or someone you know has a fever and it feels like you are "burning up," you can remember these words: "Lord, listen to my prayer; let my cry for help come to you. Do not hide from me in my time of trouble. Pay attention to me. When I cry for help, answer me quickly. My life is passing away like smoke, and my bones are burned up with fire" (Ps. 102:3 NCV).

And when someone is so sick they feel like they might die, you can remind them of Ps. 116:1-8 where it says: I love the Lord, because he listens to my prayers for help. He paid attention to me, so I will call to him for help as long as I live. The ropes of death bound me, and the fear of the grave took hold of me. I was troubled and sad. Then I called out the name of the Lord. I said, "Please, Lord, save me!" The Lord is kind and does what is right; our God is merciful. The Lord watches over the foolish; when I was helpless, he saved me. I said to myself, "Relax, because the Lord takes care of you." Lord, you saved me from death (Ps. 116:1-8 NLT).

Keeping God's Laws

The Bible says obeying God's laws is very important to stay healthy (Deut. 7:15; Ex. 15:26; Ex. 23:25-26). When King Jeroboam's son got sick, the king sent his wife to Shiloh (where the Israelites worshiped in those days) to ask a prophet what God said about the sickness. The prophet, whose name was Ahijah, told her that King Jeroboam had not followed God's laws and their son would die (1 Kings 14:1-12).

King Hezekiah also knew how important it was to follow God's laws. When he thought he was dying, he prayed to God, and after that the prophet Isaiah came to tell Hezekiah God was going to heal him (Isa. 38:1-5, 16-17; 2 Kings 20:1-6).

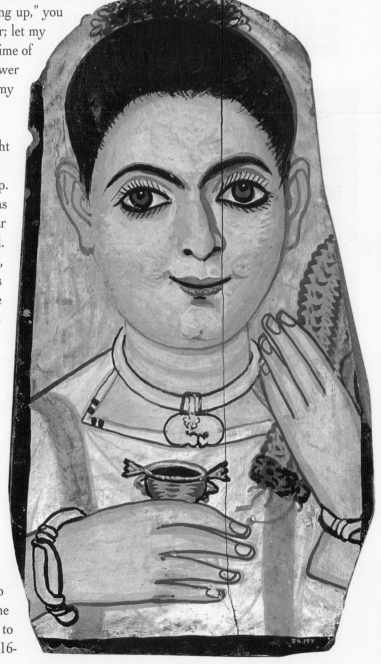

Picture of a girl from Roman times from Fayyum, Egypt (visualphotos.com)

95

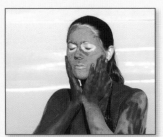

A woman covering her face with special mud at the Dead Sea. Since ancient times, people have known the mud has healthy minerals in it
(Shutterstock)

Job's Spring near the Sea of Galilee. An ancient folktale says that the biblical Job was healed by this water
(Courtesy of Eva Marie Everson)

The Roman hot springs of Tiberias, where people have come to bathe for their health since biblical times
(Todd Bolen/BiblePlaces.com)

Some of God's laws might have helped sickness from spreading, even before people knew about germs and infection. For example, when Miriam got the skin disease, God told Moses to keep her away from everyone for seven days outside their camp in the wilderness (Num. 12:14-15) until she got better.

As we can see from the stories about Ahijah and Isaiah, the Lord's prophets had something to do with healing. For example, the prophet Isaiah told the king's servant what kind of medicine to give him. Another story is about Naaman, an army officer from Syria, a country to the north of the Holy Land. When he got leprosy, his Israelite serving girl told him that the prophet Elisha could help him. Elisha was glad to do that, because that way he could show a person who did not know about God that God could heal the sick. Elisha did tell Naaman to do something special – to wash in the Jordan River. But even though washing is very important for health, Naaman soon realized that it was God, not the Jordan River water, which cured him. Still, he brought quite a bit of earth from the Holy Land back to his own country (he needed two mules to pull it!) after he got better (2 Kings 5:17). Some people still bring a little earth or water from the Holy Land home with them after their visit.

Sin and Healing

Near the Jordan River (where John the Baptist baptized Jesus and many other people), archaeologists found a grave with 30 skeletons of men, women and children. They could tell from the bones that several of the people had been sick. Perhaps the people came there to wash in the Jordan the way Naaman the Syrian had, and then to be baptized. They probably also felt that they were washing away their sins and God was forgiving them if they were baptized in the Jordan – the Bible says that if people sinned, they would get sick, and if God forgave their sins, they would get better. That is why a man in Capernaum who could not walk got well when Jesus said to him "your sins are forgiven" (Matt. 9:2).

Some people believed that certain sins, such as hatred and gossiping, could make you sick. In the book of Acts 12:23, we read that King Herod Agrippa did not give praise to God, and so he got sick with worms and died.

After King Ahaziah of Israel fell off his balcony and hurt himself, he wanted to ask a false god whether he would get better, and Elijah came to tell him God would not heal him because he had gone to a false god, which was also a sin (2 Kings 1:2-16).

Sometimes sicknesses involved bad spirits called demons, like in the story of the little boy who had fits and was deaf in Mark 9:25-26. Sickness and demons often appear together in ancient writings. Jesus gave the disciples "power and authority over demons and to heal all diseases" (Luke 9:1 NLT).

Keeping Children Healthy

Parents always worry about their children, especially about their health. But in ancient times it was probably an even bigger worry than nowadays because, as we said, people in those days didn't know as much about medicine as we do. The Gospels often mention Jesus healing children. Many parents probably brought their children to Jesus to bless them so they would stay healthy, or to make them better. In addition to Talitha, Jesus also healed a little girl who had a demon (Matt. 15:21-28), the boy who had seizures and couldn't talk (Mark 9:17-29), and the royal official's son from Capernaum (John 4:46). Some priests used to fast every Wednesday, believing that not eating was a special way of asking God to help keep children free of a disease called *askara*, which may have been diphtheria, a serious throat disease.

The hot springs of Hamat Gader in the mountains overlooking the Sea of Galilee. Tradition says Paul the Apostle bathed here for his health
(Shutterstock)

There were special customs about how to take care of newborn babies. The prophet Ezekiel says people used to wash a newborn baby with water and rub its body with salt. Today we know that salt is an antiseptic (something that helps keep disease away); for example, bathing in the Holy Land's Dead Sea, which is full of salt, is good for the skin. An ancient writing from around the time of Jesus says newborn babies should be given a bath in wine – nowadays we know that wine can also help keep germs away.

These days, newborn babies are sometimes put in incubators, a special warm crib, when they need special care. Around the time of Jesus, people were taught to keep babies warm, especially during the first seven days after they were born.

Some of the things mentioned in ancient writings that were most dangerous for children are bee stings and scorpion bites. People must have been bitten by snakes quite often (in Acts 28:5, Paul got a snake bite), because 2 Kings 18:4 says the Jerusalem Temple had a bronze statue of a serpent that the Lord had told Moses to make many centuries before. Anyone bitten by a snake could get well just by looking at that statue (Num.21:9). But King Hezekiah destroyed the serpent because the people started worshiping it as if it were a god (2 Kings 18:4).

The spring in Jericho, one of very few places where the bushes called balsam grew. The plant was used for health and beauty (Shutterstock)

What Made People Sick in Bible Days?

The Bible and other ancient sources sometimes mention people having very bad stomachaches: Elijah prophesies that King Jehoram would have a very terrible stomach disease (2 Chron. 21:15). King Herod Agrippa's "worms" (Acts 12:23) would have given him a terrible stomachache. His grandfather, King Herod the Great, also had "worms," according to the historian Josephus. The worms in these stories are not the kind in your garden that help plants grow. They are parasites, which are tiny creatures that live off of other animals, even human beings. Archaeologists looked through a microscope at ancient material they found underneath a toilet made of stone (in the part called the cesspit) in the oldest part of Jerusalem, the City of David. They found two kinds of parasites that must have been inside of peoples' stomachs thousands of years ago!

A bronze bell found in ancient Timnah (Gen. 38:12; Judges 14:5). People who believed magic could cure illness rang bells like this to "chase away" sickness
(IAA)

Pilgrims at baptism in the Jordan River, where Jesus was baptized by John and Naaman the Syrian was healed (2 Kings 5:1-15)

Statue of a snake combined with Jesus on the cross, at Mount Nebo, where Moses saw the Promised Land. Moses healed people of snakebites using a "fiery serpent" (Num. 21:4–9) and so the snake became a symbol of healing
(Courtesy of Miriam Feinberg Vamosh)

Sage, a plant used to heal aches and pains for thousands of years. One legend says Mary drank sage tea before she gave birth to Jesus

Fevers are one of the most common conditions mentioned in the Bible and in ancient writings from Bible times. We already learned how Jesus healed Peter's mother-in-law of a fever. Paul the Apostle healed a fever in the father of a man named Publius, who may have been the chief Roman leader of a community Paul witnessed to (Acts 28:8). Job, who had many sicknesses, also had a fever (Job 30:30). One ancient sage named Abaye, who lived in Babylonia, said he learned many different kinds of cures from his stepmother. For a one-day fever, he said, give the patient water. But if you lived in Abaye's day and had a fever for more than three days, he might have told you to put a chicken on your head and then dunked you in a river. The dunking would have cooled you off, but no one today can imagine how the chicken would have helped.

The Doctor Is In

Healing and saving a life is the most important thing you can do. Not only could the healthy person then go back to living a normal life; it also meant someone could go back to work and support their families. So doctors were very important. Doctors also need God to help them in their work. The wise man called Ecclesiasticus, who lived about 200 years before Jesus, said sick people should go to a doctor and the doctor would ask God what to do (Ecclus. 38:12-14).

The Bible says King Asa, who had a disease of the feet, died because he asked only doctors to help him and did not ask God (2 Chron. 16:11-12). When Jesus taught about why he spent time with people others thought were sinners, he compared them to sick people who need a doctor (Matt. 9:12).

Some ancient writings say people went to the doctor's house to see him; others said the doctor came to their house. But when the sages were talking about the prayer for healing in Ps. 6, one of them said they once had to wait seven hours to see the doctor. If that happened often, no wonder people took the sick to marketplaces (Mark 6:56) for Jesus to touch them, or into the street (Acts 5:15) for Peter to heal them.

Paul starts his letter to the Colossians with "Luke, the beloved physician," which is how we know that Luke was a doctor – the only doctor mentioned by name in the Holy Scriptures.

Medicines

People in Jesus' day used all kinds of things for medicine – some we still use and some we definitely would not! For example, Mark 8:23 tells about Jesus healing a blind man by spitting on the man's eyes. When Jesus healed the blind man in Jerusalem, he also spit in the mud and put the mud on the man's eyes. That is something no healer would do today, but using spit as part of a medicine to put on the eyes is also mentioned in the ancient book we have mentioned called the Talmud.

Doctors made their own medicines, mostly from plants (Ezek. 47:12). In the picture on page 94, you will see a child's shirt with tiny "bags" around the bottom. His or her mother would have made these to fill with herbs that were believed to keep children healthy. The Bible says a plant called hyssop (Num. 19:18) could be used to purify people (to make them feel clean in their faith) who had certain illnesses or who had come into contact with things the Bible said were harmful (Lev. 13). People also took hyssop when they had worms.

A group of Jewish men called the Essenes, who lived mainly in the desert in the time of Jesus, used "roots and medicinal stones" to heal people. At Qumran, near the Dead Sea, you can see a cave where archaeologists discovered a jar of very expensive perfume that may have also been used in healing. It was called balsam and perhaps it is what the prophet Jeremiah called "balm" (Jer. 51:8 NIV). The balsam plant was raised nearby at Ein Gedi and at Jericho. The ancient sages advised people who had an ear disease to place a piece of cloth soaked in balsam oil in their ear.

Honey was also considered a medicine. Some wise men thought honey was not good to put on a wound, but said eating honey after a meal was good for the eyes.

And while a snake bite could kill someone, snakes were also connected with healing. Some ancient people would pray to a Greek god called Aesclepius who was symbolized by a snake. Thre was a temple to Aesclepius at the site of the Pool of Bethesda before the time of Jesus, but people continued to come there when they were sick (John 5:1-3). To this day, a snake is used to represent the profession of medicine. Some people say snakes represented getting well, because snakes shed their skin and become "like new." Others point out that a little snake venom (poison) was also a cure for some sicknesses.

Some medicines did not help at all, sometimes because they were the result of superstitions (beliefs people had because of ignorance or fear), like putting a chicken on your head to cure a fever. Another superstition was that if you could not see at night, you should take seven pieces of raw meat from seven different houses, nail them to your doorpost, and let your dog chomp off the meat and eat it at the city dump.

People put bandages on injuries and sores, just like we do today (Isa. 1:6; Ezek. 30:21). Jesus told a parable about a Samaritan man who helped an injured man by bandaging his wounds (Luke 10:33-34). People did not use the same medicines we use – the Samaritan man put wine and oil on the bandages he made. Other bandages were made with wheat, caraway seeds, beeswax or reeds. Dried figs mixed with oil were also put on wounds – Isaiah suggested this for King Hezekiah when he had a sore (2 Kings 20:7). Sweet-smelling myrrh, which comes from a tree, was brought by the Three Kings of the East to the baby Jesus (Matt. 2:11), and it was also used in healing. Mark 15:23 says that when Jesus was suffering on the cross, he was given "wine mixed with myrrh," which may have been a painkiller.

Pouring oil on your skin and rubbing it in was good for you when you were sick. This was called "anointing" and was originally a way of putting on medicine (Mark 6:13; James 5:14).

The logo of the Israel Medical Association, above, uses biblical symbols. The snake, as you learned in this chapter, represents healing, while the seven-branched candelabrum, which gave light in the Temple, and the date palm symbolize the Holy Land
(Courtesy of the Israel Medical Association)

A woman drawing water from Jacob's Well (John 4:5-15) in the ancient biblical city of Shechem (Photo: American Colony, courtesy of the Eretz Israel Museum, Tel Aviv, Eilon Collection)

Figs were used to heal sores (2 Kings 20:7) and to make people feel stronger
(Shutterstock)

Water as Medicine

Some wise people already knew in ancient times that washing is very important to stay healthy. One story tells about a rabbi named Huma who used to keep a jug of water ready for anyone who wanted to wash their hands. He would say "whoever needs let him come [and wash his hands] to save his life from danger." The Bible says that when people had a skin disease, they had to wash their clothes (Lev. 13:6, 34) and themselves (Lev. 14:8-9).

Josephus mentions the hot baths of Tiberias, a city on the Sea of Galilee, as a cure. The people whom Jesus healed around the Sea of Galilee probably heard about him when they came to the healing natural hot springs of Tiberias. People still come to the hot baths there for relaxation and to feel better and healthier. King Herod also bathed in the hot springs at Callirhoe, which is on the eastern side of the Dead Sea.

Food

Certain kinds of food were said to be good for your health, like honey. Abaye's mother, who knew a lot about medicine, said a baby should be given an egg in a special mixture of sour milk, bread and salt. If someone fainted, some people believed a dried date or a fig would make them feel better. Fish especially was served to sick people to help them get better.

Since ancient times, people have known that fish is a healthy food
(Shutterstock)

Hands-on Healing

Today doctors have all kinds of medical equipment to find out what's wrong with you and to try to make you healthy. In Bible times, the most important "equipment" healers had were their hands. Jesus touched the eyes of blind men to heal them (Matt. 9:29; Matt. 20:30-34; Mark 8:23) and also healed Peter's mother-in-law by touching her. People wanted to touch Jesus because they knew his touch would heal them (Luke 6:19), people brought their babies to Jesus to touch (Luke 18:15), and Jesus healed some sick people in Nazareth by touch (Mark 6:5).

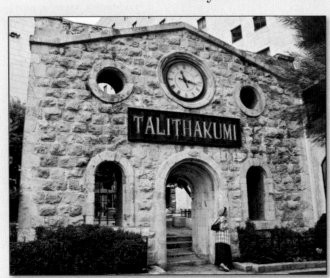

The entrance to an old orphanage in Jerusalem called "Talitha Kumi" – named after the words Jesus spoke to the young girl he healed in Capernaum (Mark 5:41). The old building was mostly torn down, but the front with this sign can still be seen in downtown Jerusalem

Breathing

When God created the first human being, Adam, the Bible says God breathed life into Adam's nose (Gen. 2:7). We can remember this when we read about how Elisha saved the boy from the Galilee town of Shunem. First, he prayed to God to heal the boy. Then the Bible says Elisha "put his mouth on the child's mouth, his eyes on the child's eyes, and his hands on the child's hands" (2 Kings 4:32-34). Some people say God gave Elisha the wisdom to know about one of the quickest ways we know today to save lives: When a person has stopped breathing, we can help them start again by breathing into their mouth, which is called CPR.

Visiting the Sick

Visiting the sick is something you can do to help someone feel better. Around the time of Jesus there was a special group of people who got together to make sure that sick people had visitors. When studying the Bible verse that commands people to "walk after the Lord your God" (Deut. 13:4, NKJV), ancient wise men around the time of Jesus said "Just as [the Lord] visited the sick, so too, we should visit the sick."

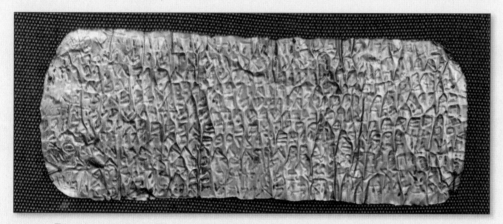

This golden plaque, about 1,500 years old, from Lebanon or Syria, calls on the name of God ("I am who I am") and eleven angels to take an evil spirit away from a woman or a girl named Klara
(Bible Lands Museum Jerusalem)

"Magic"

Did you know that the famous "magic word" abracadabra actually comes from the ancient language people spoke in Jesus' day – Aramaic, and it means something like "I will do what I say"? The Bible forbade the use of magic, and warned people against doctors who thought they were healing by using magic. In the story of King Asa going to doctors, the Bible meant he had gone to foreign doctors who used magic, and that is why he died. King Hezekiah destroyed the snake statue because it was believed to be forbidden magic. People tried to use all kinds of magic spells, especially when they were sick, and it was very hard for their leaders to persuade them not to. One thing many people did was to wear a piece of jewelry called an amulet that sometimes contained various words or Bible verses. We hope we always rely on God's word, because God's word has power, but it's not magical.

Activities

Make a Get-well Card

Pretend Talitha is a friend of yours and write her a get-well card in the space below. In the pocket at the back of this book, you'll find another card just like this one that you can use to send get-well wishes to anyone you know who is sick.

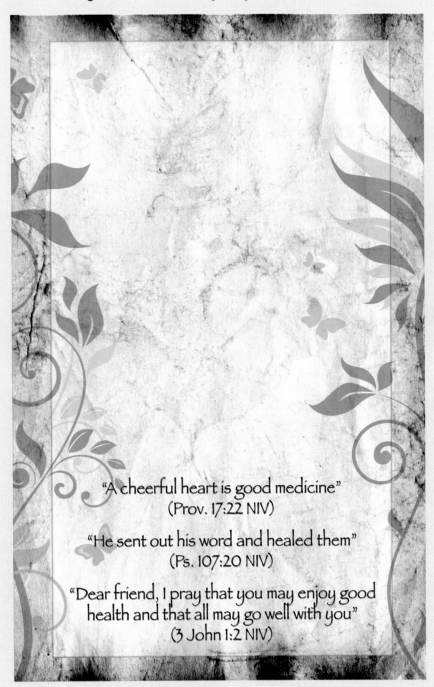

"A cheerful heart is good medicine"
(Prov. 17:22 NIV)

"He sent out his word and healed them"
(Ps. 107:20 NIV)

"Dear friend, I pray that you may enjoy good health and that all may go well with you"
(3 John 1:2 NIV)

Fix Up the Mix-up

The following pictures tell the story of Elijah healing the widow's son (1 Kings 17:17-24). But they are not in the order of the story. Read the story with family and friends and then figure out which of the pictures below comes first, second, third and fourth. Mark the pictures with numbers, 1-4. You can color them, too!

Chapter 10
Worship

Abraham and the Idols

When Abraham was young, he lived with his family in a city called Haran. Here, Abraham's father Terah had a shop where he made and sold statues of false gods called idols. In those days, the people of Haran did not know about the Lord, and believed the idols could answer their prayers. They would come to Terah's shop and pay lots of money to buy the most beautiful idols he had. So Terah grew very rich and important. Because he had many things to do for the ruler of their city, King Nimrod, he would often leave Abraham in charge of his idol store.

But Abraham always had a feeling that these silent statues of wood or stone had no power at all. He thought about this a lot, but he was not sure what he, a very young man, could do about it.

One morning, Abraham's father came in, dragging a brand-new idol so big he needed the help of two of his servants to stand it up. Terah said proudly to Abraham: "Don't you think it's the finest idol I've ever made?"

Abraham did not know what to say, so he agreed that it was a fine idol indeed. Then his father left and went about his business of being one of King Nimrod's noblemen.

After a while, a man came in to the idol store. "I am looking for the finest idol in the land," he said to the young man. The man looked behind him to the display of idols – big ones, small ones, idols of wood, stone and metal, women idols, men idols and children idols. But the new one that Terah had brought in that morning really stood out from the crowd.

It was statue of a man, seated on a throne. The stone was as smooth as silk, white with pale red and gold lines, and there were thin pieces of real gold over the eyebrows and precious stones for eyes. One arm was slightly raised and Terah had made a hole in the idol's fist to hold a beautiful bronze scepter – the rod a king holds as a sign of his power. The customer could have the scepter if he paid a little extra.

"Aha!" the man said. "That's exactly the one I want! Where's the scepter? I want to buy that, too."

But then Abraham he said to the man: "Excuse me for asking, sir, but how old are you?"

"I am very old – 50 years old. Why on earth would you ask me such a question?" the customer answered.

"Because, sir, I can't understand how a man 50 years old would pray to a statue that is only one day old!"

The man sputtered, and muttered, and huffed, and puffed. But he could not think of a single thing to say, so he pretended to be too insulted to speak, turned on his heel and marched out.

Later that day, a woman came into the idol store. She was carrying a plate with a small heap of flour. "I am too poor to buy a statue," she said. "But I want them to know that I care about them. So this morning I got up very early and ground this flour to give to the idols. Will you please give it to them?"

Abraham felt very sorry for the woman for working so hard and thinking a stone statue could care. So he took the plate of flour and said nothing but "Thank you, auntie."

But after the woman left, he had an idea. He looked around behind the shop until he found a big stick. After breaking it in two over his knee, he placed half in the hand of the big idol. Then he took other part of the stick and smashed all the other idols until only broken pieces of stone and wood were left.

Luckily, no other customers came in that day. Later, his father returned from his princely business. When Terah saw the idols smashed into bits he gasped, placed his hand over his heart and looked like he was going to faint.

"What have you done?" Abraham's father shouted at him.

Abraham had practiced his speech all afternoon. "A woman came into the store with flour to give the idols," Abraham said quietly. "When they saw it, the large idol you made yesterday said: 'I must eat first.' Then a smaller idol said: 'No, I must eat first!' They all started fighting! Then, the big idol took that rod and smashed all the others to pieces."

Terah answered him: "Are you making fun of me, my son? I made this idol myself. It can't do any of those things."

Abraham answered, "If it can't do these things, why do people worship them?"

When his father could not answer, Abraham became even braver and said: "These idols have mouths but they do not speak, ears but they do not hear, eyes but they do not see, legs but they do not walk. They are not god. Only the Lord is God, and sees everything we do and walks with us everywhere we go."

Terah knew Abraham was right. He did not know what he would say to King Nimrod, who did not know the Lord, but Terah knew his world would never be the same, thanks to his son Abraham, who told him the truth.

This story is based on an ancient legend (Genesis Rabba 38:13 and the Book of Jashar)

"Worship the Lord in all his holy splendor. Let all the earth tremble before him" (Ps. 96:9 NCV)

Mount Carmel, where Elijah called the Israelites back to the Lord (1 Kings 18)

Mosaic of grapes at the ancient church at Shiloh, where there were grapevines in Bible times (Judges 20:21) and where the Israelites set up the Lord's Tabernacle for the Ark of the Covenant (Josh. 18:1; Jer. 7:12) (Courtesy of Ancient Shiloh)

Above: Ancient Shiloh
Below: The round "high place" at Megiddo (Armageddon) where the ancient Canaanites worshiped. God said all such places had to be destroyed (Deut. 12:2)
(Todd Bolen/BiblePlaces.com)

Our story in this chapter is based on an ancient legend about Abraham which people thought up because they wanted to imagine how he came to believe in one God when the people around him still believed in many gods. We call Abraham a patriarch, which means the father of a very, very large family – you might say that everyone can look back at Abraham as the first person who believed in one God (Acts 7:2).

Abraham's grandson Jacob had twelve sons, who became patriarchs of the Twelve Tribes. When the Twelve Tribes came into the Holy Land, they found that the people living there believed there was a god in charge of bringing the wind and making it rain, and a goddess in charge of making sure animals and people had babies and that their fruit trees had fruit on them. But Moses, the leader of the Twelve Tribes, told them God did not want them to worship these gods, which he said were "made by people, gods made of wood and stone, that cannot see, hear, eat, or smell" (Deut. 4:28, NCV).

At a place in Israel called Mount Carmel, Elijah the prophet showed everyone that these gods were false gods. This is one of the most exciting stories in the Bible, and people often go to Mount Carmel to read it, right where it happened. You can find the story in 1 Kings 18.

God wanted the Israelites to worship Him in one special place in the Holy Land – a place God said He would choose (Deut. 14:23). The first place God chose in the Holy Land was called Shiloh. You can still visit Shiloh and see the place where the special tent called the Tabernacle stood. Inside the Tabernacle was the Ark of the Covenant, which held the big pieces of stone on which the Ten Commandments were carved (1 Kings 8:9) and other very important items (Heb. 9:4). It was at Shiloh where Hannah, the mother of Samuel the prophet, prayed to have a child (1 Sam. 1:3-20). Later, Hannah brought Samuel to Shiloh to help the priests serve God in the Tabernacle.

Shiloh is a good place to think more about why God wanted people to worship in one place. Some people think it was because going to one place would help everyone remember that there is only one God.

Of course, we know we can worship the Lord wherever we are. God fills the whole earth, heaven and beyond (1 Kings 8:27), as King Solomon said when he finished building the First Temple in Jerusalem and prayed to God to take care of it. Ezekiel the prophet also talked about how people could find God everywhere. Ezekiel said God would be like "a little sanctuary in the countries where they shall come" (Ezek. 11:16 KJV). (A sanctuary means a holy place.)

One special way to serve God in Bible times was to be a Nazirite, which means "separate." If you were a Nazirite, you made especially serious promises to God called vows. Sometimes your parents made those vows for you, like Samuel's mother made for him. For example, Samuel's mother promised God he would not cut his beard (1 Sam. 1:11), and so we think Samuel might have been a Nazirite. John the Baptist, who did not drink wine, might also have been a Nazirite (Luke 7:33). Like Samuel, John was

This inscription (writing carved into stone) was found in ancient Jerusalem. Written in Greek, it came from a synagogue (see page 111) from the time of Jesus. It says that people studied God's commandments there and that needy people could spend the night there (IAA)

born after his mother could not have children for a long time. Another boy who grew up as a Nazirite in the Bible (and whose mother also could not have children for a long time) was Samson. An angel told his mother not to drink wine while she was pregnant with him (Judges 13:7), which was one of the rules for Nazirites (Num. 6:1-8). Samson also had very long hair, which meant he was following another rule for Nazirites – not to cut their hair.

If you lived in those days and were a Nazirite, everyone could guess it because of your long hair. In those days, the only other people who had long hair would have been rich people, because it was so hard to take care of they needed a servant to help them.

Copies of holy objects that were in the Ark of the Covenant (Ex. 25:16; Hebrews 9:3–4) (Todd Bolen/BiblePlaces.com)

Hearing God's Word in the Wilderness

When the Tribes of Israel were wandering in the wilderness of Sinai, before they came into the Promised Land, God explained His laws to them through Moses. The Bible says that when Moses spoke to the people about God's laws, children should be there to hear them together with their parents. After the Israelites came into the Holy Land and became farmers, God told them they should thank Him for a good harvest by bringing some of it to the Tabernacle. That was called a sacrifice. By giving up something they had worked hard for, people were showing they trusted God to always give them what they needed. And when people thanked God in that way, He said the whole family should eat a special meal together at the place God chose (Deut. 14:23). That time became the chance for parents and children to worship together.

Moses also told the people that every seven years they should gather in the place God chose "so that they can listen and learn to respect the Lord your God and carefully obey everything in this law" (Deut. 31:12 NCV). Before Moses died, he sang a beautiful song to the Israelites, which appears in the book of Deuteronomy, chapter 32. In it, he tells about the good things that will happen to people as well as the bad. After he finishes, he tells everyone: "Pay careful attention to all the words I have said to you today, and command your children to obey carefully everything in these teachings" (Deut. 32:46 NCV).

View of the full-size model of the Tabernacle (Ex. 25) that you can visit at Timna Park in southern Israel (Becky Weolongo Booto/BiblePlaces.com)

Mount Sinai, where God gave Moses the Ten Commandments (Ex. 19)
(Todd Bolen/BiblePlaces.com)

Parents were to repeat the word of God over and over to their children (Deut 6:7; 11:18-19). King David said God Himself taught children to praise Him (Ps. 8:2). Jesus used King David's words when children called out to him in the Temple and people asked him whether he heard what they were saying. "Jesus answered, 'Yes. Haven't you read in the Scriptures, 'You have taught children and babies to sing praises'?" (Matt. 21:16 NCV).

Worship in the Temple

As time went on, the Israelites came into the Promised Land and built the Temple in Jerusalem, where God said people should go to worship. They worshipped in the magnificent Temple for more than 300 years, until an army from the kingdom of Babylon destroyed it in 586 BC.

Worship in the Temple meant, for example, if you were a farmer, giving up an animal you had raised, as well as some of your grain, wine and oil to show God you were grateful for a good harvest. People also brought sacrifices to the Temple to show they were sorry for something bad they had done, or just to praise God. You could also give away some of your money to help the poor and to support the priests who worked in the Temple.

A seven-branched candelabrum, called a menorah, part of the mosaic floor of the ancient synagogue of Susya. God told people to make such a menorah for the Tent of Meeting (Ex. 25:31-40), and a golden menorah stood in the Temple in Jerusalem that Jesus knew
(Shutterstock)

Many years after the Babylonians destroyed the First Temple, it was rebuilt. But then, the Romans came and destroyed it again! During that time people began to realize how important it was to show God they were grateful to Him or sorry for their sins by giving something up to help the needy. That is called charity. In Hebrew charity is called *tzedakah*, which means "the right thing." Learning that word helps us understand that it is something God wants us to do. (You will see a special project about charity in the activity section of this chapter.) How you feel about giving is very important. Jesus praised the poor widow for giving everything she had (Mark 12:41-44). Whatever you give, you should be happy about doing it "for God loves a cheerful giver" (2 Cor. 9:7 NKJV). Paul also reminded the Corinthians that Ps. 112:9 promises that God will bless a person who gives freely to the poor.

We have talked about how Jesus listened and asked questions of the teachers in the Temple (Luke 2:46). He was probably sitting with them in the outer courts of the Temple, where people were always walking around, looking at the large and beautiful buildings, giving charity, listening to teachers, selling the animals that would be offered as sacrifices and changing money from their home countries into the special coins used in the Temple. The idea that God's holy house looked like a marketplace made Jesus very angry, as John tells us (John 2:14-16). Jeremiah the prophet, who lived during the time before the First Temple was destroyed, was also angry about this (Jer. 7:11).

The clothing of the High Priest, shown in the model of the Tent of Meeting in Timna Park in southern Israel
(Todd Bolen/BiblePlaces.com)

Look on page 130 to see how the Second Temple looked. We know from the ancient book called the Mishnah that children usually could not go into the inner courtyard of the Temple, in front of the most sacred part, which was called the Holy of Holies. The one time that boys could go inside and stand in the more holy part was when a choir of Levites, the men who conducted the Temple services, would sing songs of praise to God.

Then the boys were allowed join the choir.

The Levite choir stood on a platform, with the boys standing on the ground in front of them. They were only tall enough to come up to the men's knees, so probably not everyone could see them, but their voices were so sweet that the men in the choir would sometimes feel jealous.

Ruins of the synagogue at Capernaum, where Jesus preached and healed (Luke 4:31–36)

The ancient teachers discussed what age children should be before they start coming to the Temple. Some said it was as soon as they were old enough to ride on their fathers' shoulders, and others said they should be a little older – old enough to walk alongside their father into the Temple. We can picture children in the Temple courtyard singing, because Matthew tells us about children in the Temple courts, who sang praises when they saw Jesus perform healing miracles (Matt. 21:15), as mentioned above.

Synagogues

Even before the Second Temple was destroyed in 70 AD, people used to gather in their towns and villages to study the Holy Scriptures, and also to pray (Matt. 6:5). As time went on, they built a special building to do this. It wasn't grand like the Temple, and people didn't make sacrifices or hold big, colorful ceremonies like they did in the Temple. But it was, as Ezekiel the prophet described it, their "little sanctuary" and it became the most important place in town.

Decorated stone in the synagogue of Korazim, a Galilee town where Jesus preached and made miracles (Matt. 11:21)

The synagogue was a place where people gathered (the word "synagogue," which comes from the Greek language, means "place of gathering"). That is why Jesus taught and performed miracles in synagogues in Galilee (Matt. 12:9).

Luke tells us about Jesus reading from the book of Isaiah in his hometown synagogue in Nazareth (Luke 4:16-19). We can imagine that when Jesus was growing up in Nazareth, he may have read Scripture in the synagogue, as boys were allowed to do. But children may not have taken part in the synagogue services very often. An important leader named Eleazar Ben Azariah, who lived some years after the time of Jesus, said he knew men came to the synagogue to learn and women to hear (the word of God), but wondered what children were there for. He decided their parents brought them "for a reward." What did he mean by that? Perhaps he meant they would receive a reward (a blessing) for making sure their children heard God's word. That is one of the most important things parents can do for their children, from Bible days right up till today.

In Nazareth, you can visit this underground room, which marks the place where Jesus preached and read from Scripture in the town synagogue (Luke 4) (Shutterstock)

Activities

Make a list of some things you are thankful for and write one on each line. In the box next to the line, draw a little picture that shows the thing you are thankful for.

Things I Am Thankful For

I am thankful for my family	

Do you know anyone who has visited the Holy Land? Ask them if there was a special place where God spoke to them when they were there. Ask them for a picture of the place and paste it below. If you have been lucky enough to go to the Holy Land yourself, did you have a special place where God spoke to you? Paste a picture of it in the frame below.

Crossword Fun

Look back at this chapter to find the answers

Across

1. Father of a very large family
5. Some false gods were made out of this
6. Abraham's father's name
7. The rod held by a king
9. The people who destroyed the Second Temple
10. The kingdom whose people destroyed the First Temple
12. Where Abraham once lived with his family
13. Another word for promise
15. In the Bible, a person who made a special promise to God

Down

2. Another word for false gods
3. Mountain where Elijah met the prophets of the false gods
4. Tent where the box holding the Ten Commandments was kept
5. King who built the First Temple in Jerusalem
6. Hebrew word for charity
8. People who lived in the ancient Land of Israel
11. "God loves a cheerful _____" (2 Cor. 9:7)
14. If you were a Nazirite, you were not allowed to drink this

Crossword puzzles created with EclipseCrossword—www.eclipsecrossword.com

Solution on page 144

Chapter 11
Care for the Needy

The Lame Boy and the King

My name is Mephibosheth and this is my story. First of all, if you are reading this in a country far away from where I was born in the land of Benjamin, you probably don't speak my language, Hebrew. And so I am going to tell you how to pronounce my name: Meh-fee-BO-sheth. My name is very important to who I am. I was called by **other names**, too, as I went through life.

My grandfather was Saul, the first king of Israel, and my father was Saul's son, Jonathan. When I was five years old, my father and my grandfather were killed in the war against the Philistines. My grandfather also fought against David, my father Jonathan's best friend. David won that war and became king.

My nanny was very afraid that after the war David's men would kill me, because I was supposed to be king after my father. So she came to Ziba, a servant my father trusted, and told him she would take me away to keep me safe. One night my nanny scooped me up in her arms and ran away with me. Even my mother didn't know where I was, but she knew I was safe because my nanny was with me.

My nanny later told me that there was no moon, it was very dark, and she was afraid to light a torch because David's men might find her. As she ran, she fell over some stones on the path and dropped me, and both my legs broke in several places! She didn't even know how badly I was hurt until we reached her brother's house. His name was Makir and he lived in the high mountains across the Jordan River. That's where I grew up.

It took a long time for my legs to heal. Meanwhile, Ziba, my grandfather's servant, took over all the lands that had belonged to my father and should have been mine. Ziba became very rich. At least he paid for the best doctors for me, although I wonder whether they did everything they could. I say that because I think Ziba would have been just as happy if I didn't get better, so then he would be able to keep everything he had taken from me.

Everyone in Makir's house knew that David had ordered the killing of seven of my uncles, Saul's sons. But my nanny thought I would be safe because even if David knew where I was, he had promised my father to take care of me.

I used to like to sit on the balcony that looked out over the great valley where the Jordan River flowed. I missed home. Some days I thought if I squinted enough I could see the mountaintop at Geva where my grandfather's palace stood. But I never thought I'd get to go back.

Because my legs never straightened out, I never could do what the other children could. I was even jealous of the young kitchen slaves, who walked every day to the spring to bring water to the cooks. But my nanny helped me grow strong in my faith. She taught me that after God gave Jacob his greatest blessing, for the rest of his life Jacob walked with a limp, like I do. I also studied the word of God every day with special teachers. A man also came to teach me how to shoot with a bow and arrow like my father had. "Someday, you can teach this to **your own son**," my nanny would tell me.

One day, Ziba showed up at Makir's house and said the king wanted to see me. So off we went. During the three days it took us to reach Jerusalem, Ziba didn't talk much – I think he was worried about how David was going to treat him. After all, he was the servant of David's old enemy Saul, and had taken over all my lands. I didn't worry because of what my nanny told me about David's friendship with my father Jonathan.

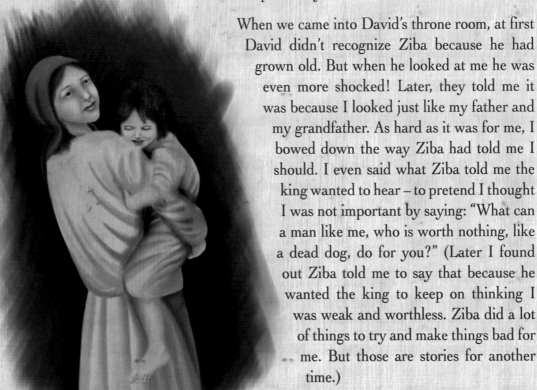

When we came into David's throne room, at first David didn't recognize Ziba because he had grown old. But when he looked at me he was even more shocked! Later, they told me it was because I looked just like my father and my grandfather. As hard as it was for me, I bowed down the way Ziba had told me I should. I even said what Ziba told me the king wanted to hear – to pretend I thought I was not important by saying: "What can a man like me, who is worth nothing, like a dead dog, do for you?" (Later I found out Ziba told me to say that because he wanted the king to keep on thinking I was weak and worthless. Ziba did a lot of things to try and make things bad for me. But those are stories for another time.)

David told me that he wanted to keep his promise to my father to take care of me, and he invited me to live in his palace as a prince like his own sons. I told him I wanted to give something to him as well. I told him about the long days I spent on my couch studying the word of God, and that I could be his teacher. At first David laughed, because I was so much younger than he was. But later, David saw how much I could teach him and he made time every day for a lesson.

When he wrote his songs of praise to God, called Psalms, he would show them to me and ask my opinion. And when people asked him whether I was a good teacher, he would say: "When I sit with my teacher (meaning me!) – **I'm ashamed** at the simple words that come out of my mouth." That's how I got the name Mephibosheth, which in Hebrew is a short way of saying "shame out of my mouth."

My troubles with Ziba may not be over, because David and I both have many enemies. But I would like the children of the future to know that when a person has disabilities, like I do, they can still do lots of good and valuable things when the people around them love and support them.

What does that mean?
Other names – Mephibosheth is called Merib-Baal in 1 Chron. 8:34

To your own son – Mephibosheth's descendants were great archers (1 Chron. 8:40)

"I'm ashamed..." – From an ancient explanation (Babylonian Talmud Berachot 4a, Shabbat 56b) for the meaning of Mephibosheth's name, connecting it to Ps. 119:6, which contain the words "put to shame" (NIV)

My troubles with Ziba – You can read in 2 Sam. 19:24-30 how Ziba made the king think Mephibosheth was his enemy, and how the king then made Mephibosheth share his land with Ziba

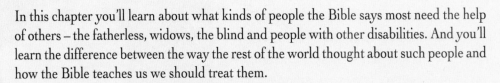
Caring for People with Special Needs

"I was eyes for the blind and feet for the lame. I was like a father to needy people, and I took the side of strangers who were in trouble" (Job 29:15-16 NCV)

The wilderness of Beersheba, where God saved the lives of Hagar and Ishmael
(Todd Bolen/BiblePlaces.com)

In this chapter you'll learn about what kinds of people the Bible says most need the help of others – the fatherless, widows, the blind and people with other disabilities. And you'll learn the difference between the way the rest of the world thought about such people and how the Bible teaches us we should treat them.

The first needy child mentioned in the Bible is Abraham's son Ishmael. Even though his mother Hagar was with him, he was in great danger, because at first she could not find any water to drink in the southern desert in the Holy Land. But then God helped her find water, which saved the lives of Hagar and her young son (Gen. 21:17-19).

Because children were weaker than grownups, it was easy for an army or powerful ruler to take them away from their parents and even sell them as slaves (Job 6:27). This could happen, for example, if their parents owed money or if they were captured during a war.

Many ancient stories tell of children being killed by kings. One such story is in the Gospel of Matthew (2:16-18), where King Herod ordered all the little boys in Bethlehem killed because he wanted Jesus dead. John the Baptist, who was about a year older than Jesus and lived in the same area where Herod sent his soldiers, was also in danger. But according to a legend, his mother Elizabeth hid him in a cave in the Judean Mountains.

Above, the entrance to the cave where some scholars believe John's mother Elizabeth hid him from the Roman soldiers; below: a picture believed to be of John holding a shepherd's staff, cut into the cave wall. (Courtesy of Dr. Shimon Gibson and Tzuba Tourism)

These days, the word "orphan" means a child who has no mother and no father. But in the Bible, the word "fatherless" is used more often than orphan. That's because in Bible times, fathers usually made a living for the whole family. If the father was gone, the whole family could starve. That's why God said He would take special care of children without fathers (Ex. 22:22-23).

Widows

In biblical days, widows (women whose husbands had died) often had to move to another place – sometimes even another country – to find a place where they could make a living, like Ruth and Naomi did (Ruth 1:1-6). In another story (2 Sam. 14:1-20), a woman comes to King David pretending to be a widow. She tells the king a story about how terrible it would be for her if having lost her husband, she would now lose her sons – it would be like losing everything on earth. She wanted King David to realize that's how he would feel if he were to lose his son Absalom, with whom he was very angry and had sent away from home.

The Blind

Blindness was common in Bible times, because people did not know about the medicines and operations we have today. As we learned in the chapter about health, Jesus healed many blind people (Matt. 9:27-29; Matt. 21:14; Luke 7:21; John 9:20; Mark 8:22-25). Because there were many blind people around them, people could more easily understand the prophet Zephaniah when he said people would "walk around like the blind" (Zeph. 1:17 NCV) because they had sinned – and to realize how hard that would be.

These people standing on a hill overlooking Bethsaida remind us of the blind man Jesus healed near that town. Once the man could see, he told Jesus: "I see people, they look like trees…" (Mark 8:24, NIV)
(David Biven/LifeintheHolyland.com)

The Lame

In Bible times, there were many people who were lame, which meant they could not walk or had trouble walking. People had accidents, just like today, but unlike today, their bones often did not heal straight. That might be what happened to Mephibosheth, the hero of the little story that started out this chapter (2 Sam. 4:4). Men who went to fight in wars came back injured, or hurt themselves at work or in other ways.

If you lived in Bible days, you would see many lame people in your town or village. So just like blindness, lameness became a symbol that you could learn from. Zechariah the prophet (Zech.11:15-17) says God will bring a shepherd. He did not mean a real shepherd for sheep, but a person who would be their leader. That seems like it would be a good thing, but then the prophet said that shepherd would not do one of his jobs – to heal the injured (Zech. 11:16). Because of that bad leader, Zechariah said, there would be many lame people and they would be saved only later.

The Inn of the Good Samaritan on the Jerusalem-Jericho road. It marks the spot of the story Jesus tells of a Samaritan who found a helpless man robbed and injured on the road, and cared for him when no one else would do so (Luke 10:30–37)
(Todd Bolen/BiblePlaces.com)

Not Being Able to Speak Well

In the time of Jesus, it was thought that if you could not speak well (for example, if you stuttered), you could not be a success. Some people went to special schools to learn how to speak well so they could earn their living making speeches. They were called orators and they took special care of their looks, because people believed that if you were good-looking on the outside, you also must be very smart. Some people said that when they first met Paul the Apostle, he did not look special and he did not speak well (2 Cor. 10:10). Moses also did not speak well (Ex. 4:10), but this did not stop him from becoming a great leader.

Living with Disabilities

Ancient documents tell us that sometimes people who had various disabilities became singers or earned a good living in other ways. For example, blind people appear in ancient stories as poets or musicians. Claudius, who was born around the time of Jesus and was emperor of Rome during the time of the first Christians, had a limp and was deaf. Yet he became the emperor of Rome, even though his family (and his enemies) thought he would not be able to.

A coin, about 1,900 years old, showing a child being presented to the Roman Emperor Trajan; the emperor wanted to show he helped hungry children after a war. (Courtesy of Classical Numismatic Group, lot no. 1016, www.cngcoins.com)

Above is a round, flat pita, the kind of bread people eat in Bible lands. Below is a stone in the ground. Can you see how much it looks like the bread? That's probably why Jesus mentioned bread and stones together when he said how important it was to take care of children
(Courtesy of Eva Marie Everson)

The Pools of Bethesda, as seen in the scale model of Jerusalem, where people with disabilities went for healing in Jesus' day (John 5:2). For the story of how Jesus healed a paralyzed man there, see Chapter 9
(Todd Bolen/BiblePlaces.com)

This type of ancient bronze coin, called a *pruta*, was like a penny – a tiny amount of money. Jesus tells about a poor widow who only had two pruta coins to her name, but still she gave them away to people less fortunate than she was
(Mark 12:42)
(IAA)

But many times widows or people who were lame, blind or had other disabilities were also poor, because they could not earn a living. So, for example, when Jesus healed the blind and the lame, or raised the widow's son, he was also saving the lives of their families, who would be able to depend on them again.

Protecting Children and People with Special Needs

Some people in ancient Rome said babies who had physical disabilities should not be allowed to live. Still, some laws in Roman times protected children. During some periods, the government used to set aside money to take care of children and make sure they had enough to eat.

Other cultures also had some laws that protected children and other people who needed to be looked after. Long before Roman times, the Babylonian ruler Hammurabi wrote a famous book of laws. At the end of that book, he wrote that he had made the laws so that stronger people would not hurt weaker people, and to keep widows and orphans safe. Another example is the Egyptian ruler named Amenhotep I who made some laws that remind us of Bible laws. For example, he said people should not laugh at a blind man, or make it harder for those who have trouble walking (see Lev. 19:14, Deut. 27:18-19).

What the Bible Says: Take Care of the Weak

The special thing about the laws in the Bible is that we are supposed to do them not because a king said so, but because God says so (Lev. 19:14). God also wanted us to remember what it was like when the people of Israel were weak – not because they were sick, but because they were slaves and had no power, and to help other weak people because of that (Deut. 24:17-18). Many other Bible verses talk about how God takes care of orphaned children (Hosea 14:3; Ps.146:9), and will help people who cannot walk or who have lost their land or their country (Zeph. 3:19-20).

Ezekiel told people God was angry with them because they did not help the weak (Ezek. 34:4). Amos also said God was angry because people did not take care of the poor and even sold them into slavery (Amos 2:6-7). Isaiah 58:6-8 also says that helping those who are weaker than you will make you stronger. James, the brother of Jesus, told the first Christians in Jerusalem to look after widows and orphans because God wanted them to (James 1:27).

Jesus also said parents should take good care of their children because God takes good care of all of us: "You parents – if your children ask for a loaf of bread, do you give them a stone instead? Or if they ask for a fish, do you give them a snake? Of course not! So if you sinful people know how to give good gifts to your children, how much more will your heavenly Father give good gifts to those who ask him?" (Matt. 7:9-11 NLT).

Have you ever noticed how when you do a good deed, it does more than only help another person? Isaiah the prophet said feeding people who are hungry and giving them clothing and shelter will heal us if we are sick, because we are doing what God wants (Isa. 58:6-8).

Because the weak and the sick had so many troubles, people also must have wondered what Paul meant when he said, "When I am weak, then I am strong" (2 Cor. 12:10 NCV) "If you are weak, then how can you be strong?" they must have wondered. That was exactly what made those words so powerful, and so people listened more closely to everything Paul had to say.

Isaiah had a vision of a good time in the future when children, both at work and at play, would be safe from dangers. As you have learned in this book, he said a child working as a shepherd (like many children did) would be able to lead a calf and a lion together (Isa. 11:6), and a child playing, even if there was a poisonous snake nearby, would not have to be afraid (Isa. 11:8).

A present-day potter at a crafts fair in Avdat in the Negev. She is showing people how she works to help them understand how the Bible compares a potter's work to God making people
(Courtesy of Miriam Feinberg Vamosh)

In the same way that people used to think children were weak and less important than adults, they also looked down on people who were lame or blind. But God cares for everyone: Jeremiah was telling us this when he said that when God brings back His people to His land, He will also bring back the blind and the lame (Jer. 31:8).

Some Bible verses have an interesting way of telling us how very important it is to take care of young creatures, who need us to protect them. A wild bear, which is a very scary animal, takes good care of her cubs and will fight to keep them safe (2 Sam. 17:8; Prov. 17:12; Hosea 13:8)

Another symbol the Bible uses when talking about how God made us and cares for us, is to picture God as a potter – a person who makes pots out of clay (Isa. 29:16; Jer. 18:l-6; Romans 9:21). If you were growing up in those days, you would have seen that when a potter makes a pot, it sometimes comes out lumpy or lopsided. But potters don't throw it out. Instead, they work on it until something good comes out of it. That is what God wanted Jeremiah to learn when he told him to go to a potter's house and watch him work: "He was using his hands to make a pot from clay, but something went wrong with it. So he used that clay to make another pot the way he wanted it to be. Then the Lord spoke his word to me: 'Family of Israel, can't I do the same thing with you?' says the Lord." (Jer. 18:4-6 NCV).

A mama bear protecting her cubs
(Prov. 17:12)
(Shutterstock)

Once in ancient times, wise men were studying Genesis 1:9, about how God created water, and they used that story to say that sometimes people are not physically perfect, but the most important thing is that they know how to praise God. They imagined that the water that God created was praising God for making it, not by using speech of course, because water can't speak. They compared God to a king who ruled over people who could not speak. But they still praised Him – in sign language and by fluttering their scarves. The story says the king then thought "if they praise me so much and they can't even speak, how much better they would praise me if they could speak." So he brought

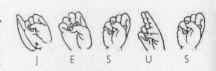

J E S U S

These letters from the American Sign Language Alphabet spell the name of Jesus in doctors who made them all able to speak. But then – guess what happened! All the people started talking to each other about how they could take over the palace and the kingdom. The wise men who told this story wanted to say that sometimes people who can't speak, praise God better than people who can.

Even though the Bible said people who were disabled could not serve as priests (Lev. 21: 21), people also realized in later times that God has a great love for people with special needs. And so they invented a special blessing you should say when you see someone who is disabled. Here it is: "Blessed are You O Lord Our God, who creates such variety in human beings!"

Activities

Have fun coloring this picture of Jesus with children

Make a Charity Box

You can save money in this box to buy food for those in need or to give to a group that helps the needy.

Use any medium-sized box with a well-fitting top for this project. Make a slit in the top to put the money in. You can also use a plastic or a glass jar without its own top, and fit a piece of cloth over the top with a rubber band or a ribbon.

Decorate your box with verses from Psalms and the Prophets about care for the needy that you learned in this chapter, and with drawings or stickers. Here are some of them for you to look up: Deut. 10:18, 14:29; 26:12-13; Ps. 22:26; Ps. 35:10; Ps. 82:3; Ps. 113:7. You can buy these, or take plain white stickers and draw your own pictures on them. You can also wrap up the whole box like a gift.

Girls in a Tel Aviv kindergarten, happy with the charity box they made
(Courtesy of Maya Dubinsky)

Chapter 12

Pilgrimage

Joshua's Journey to Jerusalem

Although Joshua was almost 13 years old, he held tightly to his father's hand. Here, at the pool of Siloam, he felt like a rock in the middle of a river of people flowing around him, as they went down to **dip into the water** and came up again, before visiting the Temple. Joshua was so excited that he had to take a deep breath – he could hardly believe it was the Feast of Tabernacles and here they were in Jerusalem!

It had taken Joshua's family six days to walk to the Holy City from their home up north in Capernaum by the Sea of Galilee. They were exhausted when they finally arrived at the little guesthouse next to the synagogue in the oldest part of Jerusalem. But they had gotten up at sunrise this morning to go to the famous pool. The tall, thin palm branches held by most of the men rose above their heads, making the crowd look like a moving forest. Joshua's father carefully cradled the special fruit – a citron that looked like a big crinkled lemon – so it would stay beautiful until the end of the feast and be a wonderful symbol of their happiness. Joshua was looking forward to the end of the holiday when his father would give it to him and his brothers and sisters to share. Papa said the citron would be a little sour, but that it always "tasted like Jerusalem" to him, and that sounded nice. It was the second day of the holiday, and like yesterday and each of the remaining six days, the day began with the festive Water-Drawing Ceremony.

"Look, look, son! Here come the priests!" Joshua's father shouted, as the crowd's murmuring rose to a roar. Joshua had grown taller since his blessing last year in the synagogue, but he still had to stand on tiptoe just to catch a glimpse of the priests. The High Priest's robe, woven with threads of gold, purple, red, sky-blue and white, was the most amazing piece of clothing Joshua had ever seen. He could not see the tiny golden bells on the fringe of his robe or the famous breastplate that had the special stones on which the names of the Tribes of Israel were written, but he could hear the bells tinkling when the High Priest passed.

"The priests have filled their golden jug with water – hurry, now we're going to follow them to the Temple!" Joshua's mother said. The air was filled now with the singing of the crowd, and the sound of the flutes and the great ram's horn trumpets, as they began to walk up the stone-paved street from the pool to the Temple. Many fathers carried small children on their shoulders, but all children who were old enough walked alongside their parents. Joshua's father carried the lamb he would give the priests for an offering, and everyone in the family who was big enough carried some part of the offerings they would give to the priests from their harvest – the grain, the wine and the oil. Joshua began to think about last year, when his family had had to give up their pilgrimage because they could not afford to go. Joshua had been blessed by the elders in the synagogue at home in Capernaum instead, but they had prayed for good things for him. And now, here he was in Jerusalem.

Suddenly, as he was daydreaming, a little knot of people, pushed between him and his family, and he felt his hand slip out of his father's. Before he knew it he was surrounded by strangers. What would he do now? How would he find his family again among thousands of people from all over the world?

There was a lot of pushing as the crowd moved forward, but people also watched out for each other in Jerusalem, and sure enough, a woman saw Joshua was in trouble. She took his hand and said: "Don't worry, young fellow. I've got you! I'll take you to the Claiming Stone and you'll be back with your family in no time!"

The Claiming Stone was a rocky open area at the top of the hill just below the Hulda Gates where people went to find anything they had lost – including their children. What a scene! Baby goats and lambs baaing, lost donkeys braying; people everywhere calling out the names of things they had lost or found. Joshua almost forgot he was lost as he watched open-mouthed while two men argued over a cloak that had been found. The man who claimed it said he could prove it was his because his wife had woven his name into the hem when she made it. People were in a hurry by now, so the cloak was quickly returned to its true owner, and the man who had tried to take it slipped away ashamed into the crowd. Joshua couldn't imagine why someone would come all the way to Jerusalem to worship the Lord, and then lie to get a robe that wasn't his. But he didn't have much time to think about this, because another stranger shook his arm. "What's your name, boy? I'll shout for you," the man said.

"I am Joshua from Capernaum," the boy answered, trying to sound brave.

"I HAVE A JOSHUA HERE. JOSHUA FROM CAPERNAUM," the man bellowed.

Before Joshua could blink three times, there was his mother! She swept him up in her arms, and Joshua made a face as she hugged him so tight he could hardly breathe. "The Lord bless you," she said to the man.

By now, the priests with the golden jug of Siloam water had disappeared into the inner Temple. But the crowd was still moving upward, and the family once more joined everyone else walking up the wide steps to the Hulda Gates, singing Psalms. As they entered the long, dim tunnel that led to the outer Temple courtyard, they all looked up at the gorgeous ceiling, covered all over with carved decorations. "No wonder this is also called the Beautiful Gate," his mother said.

When they came out of the tunnel into the Temple court, Joshua's father first gave a silver half-shekel to the priest outside the special office where people left their money offerings. "Let's meet for the evening festivities at the doorway of the Chamber of Oils in the Women's Court," he told his wife. "And take care of your mother and little brothers and sisters, Joshua," he instructed his son.

Then he left to bring their offerings to the priests. He was still carrying the family's Four Species, which he would wave before the altar, along with the other pilgrims, today and every day for the next six days.

Joshua, his mother, and his brothers and sisters spent the rest of the day walking around the outer Temple court. There was so much to see they didn't feel the time passing. "Remember how crowded we were on the street and in the tunnel coming up here? Look around you now – there are even more people here and it seems that we all have enough room. It's like a miracle!" his mother said to the children.

By late afternoon, the huge stone pillars were casting long shadows in the great walkway where some wise men sat teaching. Each teacher was surrounded by a little knot of people who were asking questions and listening to the answers as closely as they could, even though it was very noisy with everyone talking at the same time. "Look how people are trying to learn everything they can from the wise men gathered here! After being in Jerusalem, you'll all want to keep studying God's word even more when we get home," Joshua's mother said.

They listened for a while before continuing all the way around the outer court. Finally they were almost back where they had started that morning, at the gate into the Women's Court. They entered and walked across the courtyard as far as the round steps going up through the Nicanor Gates to the Court of the Israelites. Papa was probably already waiting for them, but Mama let them stop for a few more minutes at the bottom of the stairs, because she knew they would never forget the sight.

From the outer court, they had seen the smoke of the sacrifices rising straight up to the sky even though there was a breeze (people said this was a miracle). Finally, Mama pulled them away and they continued to the doorway of Chamber of Oils, where the priests kept the olive oil to light the Temple lamps.

The sun had set, but the Levites, the men who served in the Temple and helped the priests, had lit so many tall oil lamps that it still seemed like daytime. Joshua was wondering how his father would ever find them in the crowd, but he did. Mama left Joshua with his father and took the younger children up a nearby wooden stairway to a balcony overlooking the courtyard. The courtyard was now filled with men dancing and singing. The most beautiful voices of all were those of the Levites, singing beautiful hymns as they stood on the steps leading inward to the holiest part of the Temple. Some were even juggling with lighted torches. Papa grabbed Joshua and they plunged happily into the joyful circle, where they danced until the sky grew light.

What does that mean?

Dipping in the water – When people dipped in water before going to the Temple or at other special times, this was called "purifying themselves" – they were doing it because it reminded them that it was important to be "clean on the inside" before they worshipped the Lord (Acts 21:26).

An ancient road in the Valley of Elah

Celebrating in the Holy City of Jerusalem

"When he was 12 years old, they went up to the Feast,
as they always did" (Luke 2:42 NCV)

Wall painting depicting pilgrims at the
Siloam Pool in the City of David in
Jerusalem, near the actual pool itself .
(Archive of the City of David: Painting: Yael Kilemnik.
Photo: Oren Cohen)

The idea of coming to Jerusalem to worship the Lord goes all the way back to the beginning of biblical history. When the Tribes of Israel went to Mount Sinai to receive the Ten Commandments, God also told them there would be three special times to celebrate holidays (Exodus 23:14-17). One of these holidays was the Feast of Tabernacles (when Joshua, the boy in our story, finally gets to go to Jerusalem). The Bible also tells the Israelites to celebrate two other very special holidays – the Feast of Unleavened Bread (Passover) and the Feast of Weeks (Pentecost) – in a place He would choose (Deut. 12:14; 14:24). As time passed, everyone realized that the chosen place was the city on the mountaintop, Jerusalem, and began coming there to worship the Lord on these holidays and at other times, too. Making a trip to a special place for your faith is called a pilgrimage, and the people who make the trip are called pilgrims.

The Holy of Holies in the Temple, as seen in the
famous scale model of Jerusalem of Jesus' time
(Shutterstock)

These holidays are mentioned in the Gospels. For example, the verse you see at the top of this page comes from the story of the trip to Jerusalem made by Jesus and his family for the Passover festival. And of course during Passover many years later Jesus was crucified in Jerusalem.

Once, during the Feast of Weeks (Pentecost), the Holy Spirit came down from heaven and pilgrims from all over the world heard people praying in their languages, although the people praying did not know these languages before (Acts 2:1-11). And John tells us that the disciples wanted Jesus to go to Jerusalem for the Feast of Tabernacles, when the city would be full of people from all over the world (John 7:2-4).

Two Reasons to Celebrate God's Goodness

Each of these holidays combined two reasons for worship and celebration: One reason was to remember the great things God did for the Israelites and the second was to give thanks for a good harvest. Passover, for example, celebrates the great miracles God made to free the Israelites from Egyptian slavery, such as dividing the Red Sea. And since the holiday comes in the spring, it is also the time in the Holy Land when grain begins to get ripe.

A tabernacle is a special kind of house that can be taken apart easily and moved from place to place, as the Israelites did for all those years. Afterward, God told the Israelites to build tabernacles to remember those years of wandering (Lev. 23:42-43). The festival, which comes in the fall, is also the time to thank God for the fall harvest.

The symbols of the Feast of Tabernacles
(Lev. 23:40)
(Shutterstock)

Pentecost is celebrated on the 50th day after Passover, just as spring is turning into summer. (The word Pentecost means "50th day" in the Greek language.) The 50th day after Passover is also seven weeks, and so in Hebrew the holiday is called the Feast of Weeks. It was the time when God gave the Ten Commandments (Ex. 19-20) to the Israelites.

It is also just about the time that the grain is ready for harvest. But in the Holy Land, the change of seasons often brings big storms with high winds, heavy rain and hail that can ruin the grain. If that happened and the harvest was ruined, people could end up with no bread to eat. And so people began to say special prayers every day in the weeks between Passover and Pentecost and to thankfully count every day (Lev. 23:15-16) that passed. The beautiful biblical story of Ruth takes place on Pentecost.

A girl holding *matzah*, the special bread of the feast of Passover (Ex. 12:18)
(Shutterstock)

Symbols of the Holidays

Each of these holidays has special symbols. For Passover, it is the special flat bread called *matzah* that is baked without yeast, which you learned about in the chapter on food. The Bible tells us that this is how the Israelites had to bake their bread when they escaped from slavery in Egypt, since they didn't have time for the yeast to make the bread rise (Ex. 12:34, 39). Passover is also called the Feast of Unleavened Bread (Ex. 23:15; Mark 14:1; Luke 22:1; Acts 12:3; Acts 20:6).

The Feast of Weeks was celebrated when the wheat was ready for harvest, so a bundle of wheat became the holiday's symbol.

The Feast of Tabernacles, which celebrates the fall harvest, is symbolized by plants – a palm branch, a myrtle branch, a willow branch and a citron (Lev. 23:40). Many of the Seven Species of fruits of the Land

The ancient steps of the Pool of Siloam (John 9:7)
(Archive of the City of David – ancient Jerusalem. Photo: Vladimir Neichin)

This is the reverse side of the 2nd century AD silver coin shown on page 24. This side shows the Four Species from the Feast of Tabernacles, which reminded people of making pilgrimages to the Temple in Jerusalem (Courtesy of Classical Numismatic Group.www.cngcoins.com)

A copy of the seven-branched candelabrum called the Menorah that once stood in the Temple that Jesus knew. You can see this beautiful candelabrum standing in Jerusalem today

A seven-branched candelabrum in the mosaic of the Ein Gedi synagogue

of Israel (Deut. 8:8) also ripen around then and have become symbols of this holiday, like grapes, olives, dates, figs and pomegranates. In Israel, people still celebrate this holiday by building a tabernacle right outside their home and eating or even sleeping in it for seven days, like the Bible says (Lev. 23:42).

Like all the feasts in the Bible, the Feast of Tabernacles is very important to Christians. We especially remember that Zechariah the prophet said that in the future, God will want people from all over the world to come to Jerusalem to celebrate the Feast of Tabernacles (Zech. 14:16). Many Christians have already started doing this, and the Feast of Tabernacles has become a special time of Christian pilgrimage to Jerusalem.

Going to the Temple

On these three feasts, everyone who could went to the Temple in Jerusalem. People said the Temple was the most beautiful building in the whole world. Luke tells us that once when Jesus was at the Temple with his disciples: "Some people were talking about the Temple and how it was decorated with beautiful stones and gifts offered to God" (Luke 21:5 NCV). But Jesus then told people the Temple was going to be destroyed. And that is exactly what happened some years later – the Romans conquered the Jewish people and tore down the Temple. The only part of the Temple that is still standing so high today is an outer wall called the Western Wall.

In the little story that opens this chapter, Joshua and his mother began their visit to the Temple in the outer courtyard, where anyone visiting the Temple could go. Before that, his father handed in the half-shekel that every Jewish man had to donate each year to the Temple, probably at that same place where Jesus saw both the rich and the poor giving in their offerings, and praised the poor widow for giving freely all she had (Luke 21:1-4).

Joshua and his mother also went through a gate to an area where only Jewish people could go, which was called the Women's Court. Beyond that was a place called the Court of the Israelites, and even further inside, was the altar where people brought their offerings to the priests. Behind the altar rose the magnificent marble and gold building housing the holiest place of all, the special inner room called the Holy of Holies. In the room was a curtain (Heb. 6:19, 9:3) separating the most holy part from the rest, which tore all by itself when Jesus was crucified (Matt. 27:51; Mark 15:38; Luke 23:45). When Solomon built the First Temple, he put the Ark of the Covenant there. But when the First Temple was destroyed, the Ark was lost. In the Temple of Jesus' time, the Holy Spirit was in the Holy of Holies. Even after the Second Temple was destroyed, people continued to believe that Holy Spirit stayed over that place in a special way. That's why the Western Wall, the only part of the Second Temple that wasn't torn down, is holy to this very day.

As you learned, bringing gifts to God was a very important part of worship and by Jesus' time, everyone brought their offerings to the Temple in Jerusalem. People also came to the Temple to learn Scripture. Jesus taught in the Temple (Matt. 21:23; John 7:28) and so did Peter and John (Acts 4:1). People also prayed there, like Anna, who met Joseph and Mary when they brought Jesus there as a baby (Luke 2:36-37). Jesus told a story about two men who went to the Temple to pray (Luke 18:10-14). Just the feeling of being surrounded by thousands of people praying and singing to the Lord was enough to make people feel closer to the Lord God by coming to this special place in Jerusalem.

View of Jerusalem's Jaffa Gate and David's Tower, with the ancient walls lit up

Up and Up

People sang Psalms when they came to Jerusalem, especially the "Psalms of Ascent." In Hebrew these Psalms are called the "Psalms of the Steps" and people probably also sang them as they walked up the outer steps to the Temple, which is on a mountain that rises above Jerusalem's ancient valleys and is still called the Temple Mount. That reminded them that they were not only walking up steps, but feeling that they were "going up" and hopefully feeling closer to God. In Jerusalem today, archaeologists have discovered the ancient steps going up to the Temple at the Hulda Gates, and today's pilgrims like to go up these steps and sing the Psalms of Ascent.

The Kidron Valley (2 Sam. 15:23; John 18:1) at the foot of the Mount of Olives in Jerusalem, with the Tomb of Absalom. Jesus would have passed this tomb on his way to the Temple (Mark 11:11)

Giving offerings that brought people closer to the Lord, learning God's word, being with thousands of others who were in Jerusalem for those same wonderful reasons, made people happy that they had come to Jerusalem. That is just what one of the Psalms of Ascent, Psalm 122, means when it says: "I was happy when they said to me, 'Let's go to the Temple of the Lord.'" (Ps. 122:1 NCV)

Isn't it wonderful that people are still coming to Jerusalem today and worshipping there – every day, people of all faiths, from every corner of the world? We can be happy about this, too, and remember God's promise: "I will bring these people to my holy mountain and give them joy in my house of prayer...because my Temple will be called a house for prayer for people from all nations" (Isa. 56:7 NCV).

The Western Wall in Jerusalem is now a very holy place, because it is the last part of the ancient Temple that is still standing so high

Franciscan churchmen walking down the Via Dolorosa, the path Jesus followed while carrying the cross in Jerusalem

Activities

Going Up to Jerusalem
Be an ancient pilgrim – find your way up to the Holy City

Starting from Square 1 at the bottom left, take turns rolling one die and then moving your marker forward by that number of squares. If you land on the bottom of a ladder, you can take a shortcut and whiz right up to the top of it. But beware: If you land at the top of a slide, you have to tumble all the way down to the bottom of it and start again from there. First player to reach the Holy City wins!

79

80 Your camel broke its leg!

81

82

JERUSALEM

66

65

64

63

62

61

55

56

57

58

59 A rainstorm to wait out

60

42

41

40

39

38

37

31

32 An angel shows the way

33

34

35

36

18

17

16

15

14 Wheat to make bread

13

7

8

9 Yummy grapes!

10

11

12

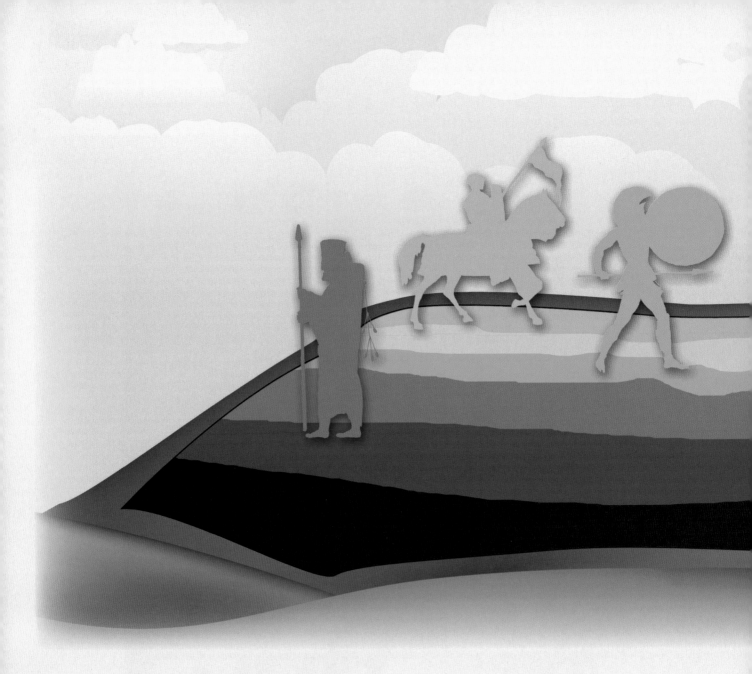

Let's Learn About a Tell

People lived for thousands of years in many of the biblical places you've been reading about in this book, such as Megiddo (Armageddon), Hazor, Beersheba and Gezer. In those days, people built their cities one on top of the other in the same place, using many of the same stones for their buildings and making their tools out of stone and clay. So even though these cities no longer exist, we know where they were because the ruins piled up to form a hill, called a tell. The tell is formed of levels that piled up at different times in history. Archaeologists are people who dig into the layers of the tell to find the ruined buildings, pots, statues and tools of all kinds (you have seen many of these in the photos and drawings in this book). After archaeologists study these things, they can teach us many things about how people lived in Bible times.

Here you see an imaginary tell. Each color and each person represents a different period in history. The most ancient period (the Canaanites) are at the bottom. At the end of this book you'll find stickers that show people wearing the typical clothing of certain periods. Place the sticker from the right period over the right person on the tell – and you'll see which level that person would have lived on.

The tell of Megiddo (Armageddon), one of the most famous in the Holy Land
(Todd Bolen/BiblePlaces.com)

137

Selected Bibliography

The Holy Bible: BibleGateway.com. Versions: NASB (New American Standard Bible); NCV (New Century Version); NIV (New International Version; NKJV (New King James Version); NLT (New Living Translation); RSV (Revised Standard Version).

Bunge, M. and Fretheim T. The Child in the Bible. Grand Rapids: Eerdmans. 2008.

Aasgaard, R. "From Boy to Man in Antiquity: Jesus in the Apocryphal Infancy Gospel of Thomas." THYMOS: Journal of Boyhood Studies. Vol. 3 No. 1 (Spring 2009): 3-20.

Aasgaard, R. "Paul as a child: children and childhood in the letters of the Apostle." Journal of Biblical Literature 126:1 (2007):129-59.

Abrams, J. Judaism and Disability: Portrayals in the Ancient Texts from the Tanach Through the Babli. Washington, D.C.: Gallaudet University Press. 1998.

Avalos H., Mecher S. and Schipper, J. This Abled Body: Rethinking Disabilities in Biblical Studies. Atlanta: Society of Biblical Literature. (2007):145-160.

Argetsinger, K. "Birthday Rituals: Friends and Patrons in Roman Poetry and Cult Classical Antiquity, Vol. 11, No. 2 (Oct. 1992): 175-193.

Ariel, Y. The Odyssey of the Third Temple. Translated and adapted by Chaim Richman. Jerusalem: G. Israel Publications and the Temple Institute. 1994.

Bar-Ilan, M. "Children's Games in Antiquity," Proceedings of the Eleventh World Congress of Jewish Studies, Jerusalem: World Union of Jewish Studies, 1994, B:I. Pp. 23-30 (Hebrew).

Bar-Ilan, M. Scribes and Books in the Second Temple Period and the Period of the Mishna and the Talmud. Ramat Gan: Bar-Ilan University. 1996 (Hebrew).

Bar-Ilan, M. "The Battered Jewish Child in Antiquity." http://faculty.biu.ac.il/~barilm/battered.html.

Bar-Ilan. "Childhood and its Status in Biblical and Talmudic Societies."Beit Mikra, 40/140 (1995): 19-32.

Borowski, O. Daily Life in Biblical Times. Atlanta: Society of Biblical Literature. 2003.

Cohen, S.J.D. The Jewish Family in Antiquity. Atlanta, Georgia: Scholars Press. 1993.

Crawford, S. 2009. The Archaeology of Play Things: Theorizing a Toy State in the 'Biography' of Objects. Childhood in the Past 2: (2009): 55-70.

Demsky, A. "Abecedaries." In The Context of Scripture-Vol. 1: Canonical Texts from the Biblical World. W.W. Hallo, ed. Leiden: Brill. Pp. 364-367.

Demsky, A. Literacy in Ancient Israel. Jerusalem: The Bialik Institute. 2012 (Hebrew).

Dixon, S., ed. Childhood, Class and Kin in the Roman World. London-New York: Routledge. 2001.

Feinberg Vamosh, M. Daily Life at the Time of Jesus. Herzliya: Palphot. n.d.

Feinberg Vamosh, M. Food at the Time of the Bible. Herzliya: Palphot. n.d.

Feinberg Vamosh. M. Women at the Time of the Bible. Herzliya: Palphot. n.d.

Fleishman, J., Studies Pertaining to the Legal Status of the Child in the Bible and in the Ancient Near East, Ph.D. diss., Bar-Ilan University, Ramat Gan. 1989 (Hebrew).

Gardner, J. and Wiedemann, J. The Roman Household: A Sourcebook. London-New York: Routledge. 1991.

Golden, M. Children and Childhood in Classical Athens. Baltimore-London: The Johns Hopkins University Press. 1990.

Grieve, J. "Jewish Health and Healing in Bible Times." Pharmacy History Australia Vol. 3 No. 31 (March 2007): 15-18.

Hadar, D. Space-Time in the Talmudic Reality: The Daily Regimen of the Jewish Family in the Mishnah and Talmud Periods. Ph.D. diss., Bar-Ilan University, Ramat Gan. 2006 (Hebrew).

Horn, C. and Martens, J. Let the Little Children Come to Me: Children and Childhood in Early Christianity. Washington, D.C.: Catholic University of America Press. 2009.

How to play knucklebones (No Author): eHow http://www.ehow.com/how_2171996_play-knucklebones.html.

Jacob, I. and Jacob, W., eds. The Healing Past: Pharmaceuticals in the Biblical and Rabbinic World. Leiden: Brill. 1993.

Janowitz, N. Magic in the Roman World: Pagans, Jews, Christians. London-New York: Routledge. 2001.

Klein, A.E. Child Life in Greek Art. New York: Columbia University Press. 1932.

Kottek, S. Medicine and Hygiene in the Works of Josephus. Leiden: Brill. 1994.

Kraemer, D. The Jewish Family: Metaphor and Memory. New York-Oxford: Oxford University Press. 1989.

Lally. M and Ardren, T. "Little Artifacts: Rethinking the Constitution of the Archaeological Infant." Childhood in the Past 1(2008): 62-77.

Malka, S. Jewish Law and Practice in the History of Clothing in the Land of Israel at the Time of the Mishna and Talmud. M.A. thesis, Bar-Ilan University, Ramat Gan. 1998 (Hebrew with English summaries).

Marcus, D. Juvenile Delinquency in the Bible and the Ancient Near East. Journal of the Ancient Near Eastern Society 13 (1981): 31-52.

Mau, A. Pompeii: Its Life and Art. Translated by Francis Kelsey. New York-London: Macmillan. 1907.

Montefiori, C.G. and Loewe, H.A. Rabbinic Anthology. New York: Schocken. 1974.

Naveh J. Early History of the Alphabet. Jerusalem-Leiden: The Magnes Press and Brill. 1982.

North, R. "Medical Discoveries of Biblical Times." In Scripture and Other Artifacts: Essays on the Bible and Archaeology in Honor of Philip J. King, M.J. Coogan C. Exum and L.E. Stager, eds. Louisville, Ky.: Westminster John Knox. 1994.

Perdue, L., Meyers, C., and Blenkinsopp, J., eds. Families in Ancient Israel. Louisville, Ky.: Westminster John Knox. 1997.

Praglin, L. "Biblical Healing." http://www.myjewishlearning.com/practices/Ethics/Our_Bodies/Illness_and_Healing/Biblical_and_Post-biblical.shtml.

Rahmani, L.Y. "Finds from a Sixth to Seventh Centuries Site Near Gaza: The Toys." Israel Exploration Journal 31 (1981): 72-80.

Rawson, B. L., ed. The Family in Ancient Rome: New Perspectives, Ithaca, New York: Cornell University Press. 1986.

Rawson, B. Marriage, Divorce and Children in Ancient Rome. Oxford: Clarendon Press. 1991.

Rawson, B. and Weaver, P., eds. The Roman Family in Italy: Status, Sentiment and Space. Oxford: Clarendon Press. 1997.

Romero, M.S. "Childhood and the Construction of Gender Identities through Material Culture." Childhood in the Past 1 (2008): 17-37.

Rosner, F. Medicine in the Bible and the Talmud: Selections from Classical Jewish Sources. Hoboken, N.J.: Ktav. 1995.

Saban, M. "Games in the Ancient World." Davar Avar, Vol. 12 (February 2008): 10-11 (Hebrew).

Safrai, S. and Stern, M., eds. The Jewish People in the First Century: Historical Geography, Political Geography, Political History, Social Cultural and Religious Life and Institutions. Philadelphia: Fortress Press. 1974.

Schipper, J. Judaism and Disability: Protrayals in Ancient Texts from the Tanach Through the Bavli. Washington D.C.: T. & T. Clark International. 2006.

Schwartz, J. "Material Culture and Rabbinic Literature in the Land of Israel in Late Antiquity: Beds, Bedclothes, and Sleeping Habits." In L.I. Levine, Continuity and Renewal: Jews and Judaism in Byzantine-Christian Palestine. Jerusalem: Dinur Center for the Study of History, Yad Ben-Zvi and Jewish Theological Seminary of America. 2004. Pp. 197-209 (Hebrew).

Shumka, L.J. Children and Toys in the World: A Contribution to the History of the Roman Family. M.A. thesis, University of Victoria, Canada. 1993.

Sparkes, B. Greek Pottery, an Introduction. Manchester: Manchester University Press. 1991.

Strauss, Y.M. Three Special Days. Jerusalem-New York: Feldheim. 2003.

Tufnell, O. Lachish III. London: Oxford University Press. 1953.

Uzzi, J.D. Children in the Visual Arts of Imperial Rome. Cambridge University Press. Cambridge-New York. 2005.

Zias, J. Death and Disease in Ancient Israel Biblical Archaeologist. (September 1991): 147-159.

Index

Want to know more?
Below, by chapter, are ancient sources for some of our stories.

Chapter 2, Education: Teaching child to swim: Babylonian Talmud, Kiddushin 29a; teachers shining like stars: Leviticus Rabba 30.

Chapter 4, Animals: David riding an oryx: Midrash Psalms 22; sea lions: Ecclesiastes Rabba 6:11; Monkeys as pets: Ecclesiastes Rabba 6:11; monkeys doing housework: Babylonian Talmud, Eruvin 31a); blessing on seeing an unusual animal, Babylonian Talmud, Brachot 58b.

Chapter 6, Milestones: Stages of life: Mishnah 5, 21; three partners in creation: Babylonian Talmud, Niddah 31a; Moses and the hot coals: Exodus Rabba 1:26.

Chapter 7, Food: Ten people invited for a meal: Eliyahu Rabba (Ish-Shalom) 18; 180,000 markets for pudding dealers: Babylonian Talmud, Baba Bathra 75b.

Chapter 8, Water: Rabbi Joshua and the rain: Midrash Psalms 117:1; rejoicing when it rains: Midrash Psalms 117:1; water is like studying Bible: Babylonian Talmud, Baba Kama 82a.

Chapter 9, Health: Gossip can make you sick: Babylonian Talmud, Shabbat 33a; Fasting to protect children from diphtheria: Babylonian Talmud, Taanit 27b; giving newborns a wine bath: Tosefta, Shabbat 12, 13; washing hands to stay healthy: Babylonian Talmud, Taanit 20b, 21a; chicken on the head and a river-dunking: Babylonian Talmud, Gittin: 97b; waiting seven hours to see the doctor: Midrash Psalms 6:5; hyssop cures worms: Babylonian Talmud, Shabbat 109a; spit as medicine Babylonian Talmud, Shabbat 108b; balsam for ear disease: Babylonian Talmud, Abodah Zara 28b; Abaye's mother on what to feed babies: Babylonian Talmud, Ketuboth 50a; dry date or fig after fainting: Lamentations Rabbah 1:2; serving fish to the sick: Babylonian Talmud, Berachot 57b; visiting the sick is important: Babylonian Talmud, Moed Katan 17b.

Chapter 10, Worship: Boys singing in the Temple choir: Mishnah, Arakhin 2, 6; boys reading scripture in synagogue: Babylonian Talmud, Megillah 23a; parents bringing children to synagogue "for a reward": Tosefta, Sotah 7, 9; boys walking alongside their fathers to the Temple: Mishnah, Hagigah 1, 1.

Chapter 11, Care for the Needy: People who can't speak praising God: Genesis Rabbah 5:1; blessing for a disabled person: Babylonian Talmud, Baba Kamma 87a.

Chapter 12, Pilgrimage: Claiming Stone: Babylonian Talmud, Baba Metzia 28b.

Answers to the game on page 14

Answers to the game on page 25

Answers to the game "Who Am I" on page 40

1. Camel; 2. Oryx; 3. Leopard; 4. Donkey; 5. Jackal; 6. Fox

Answers to the crossword puzzle on page 113

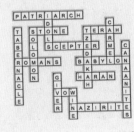